Reviews

WILD AT HEART

'This is a punch in the stomach sort of read. Dynamic, staccato sentences lead the reader into an anxiety induced state. The characters in this collection are not poignant people musing existential woes. They are people at the edge fighting for their lives! The writing aims to achieve directness and sense of urgency as well as raw honesty. Nothing is sugar coated or nuanced. The reality that hits you is elemental and solid. In every story/chapter there is a fatal meeting of a perpetrator and a victim. The violence is breath taking and racy and the amount of emotions invested are huge. If I have to choose one from the stories of would be **Tell him to Run**. Maximum impact and a fine example of the merits of unpretentious, direct writing that differentiates between the weak and tasteless sentimental and the raw humane and emotional. Very impressive.'

DEVIL'S FOOD CAKE

'Not my usual read but I am glad I did. This is a collection of short stories with dark and difficult themes. Henningham will draw you into worlds of drugs, violence and abuse in this study of human psychology and the depths of depravity, with a unique style of visceral and harrowing descriptions at times at odds with humorous insights. The familiarity of Henningham's characterisation, use of dialogue and setting mixed with situations that are alien to this reader, took me on a rollercoaster of a journey that left me feeling suitably uncomfortable, disturbed and emotional. A very clean and well formatted book made these pages fly by. I recommend this book for anyone who enjoys well written, engaging and absorbing writing.'

MASTERFUL SHORT STORIES

'This is one of the best short story collections I've ever read. I can say with all honesty that no matter what genre of work you prefer, you will miss out on some of the edgiest and best writing a reader can devour. There are five (would have eaten far more) tales of victims and perpetrators that are delivered from first person point of view. Normally, this might, in a short story, result in a thinly painted descriptive monologue, but the authors commanding style of writing delivers. You will enter the dark and often seedy world of the protagonists, you will feel their pain, frustration and fear. There are deeper messages in each of the stories, thought provoking understanding of the circumstances that cause us or the characters to behave badly, even an innocent child manifesting fears by reading the emotional undercurrents between loving and caring parents. This is definitely a must read. I am now going to work my way through the other books published by this author.'

The title sums it up

'Deliciously dark indeed. If you are looking for a quick read that will leave you enthralled then look no further. This is a collection of atmospheric tales that are definitely dark and certainly delicious.'

Engaging

'Punchy, raw and gritty - I loved these stories. These five cleverly crafted stories left me wanting more. Strictly for adults, these contain dark themes and have been written in such a way that the writing complements each story.'

Articulated in a thought-provoking manner

'Behaving Badly" turned out to be in a stark contrast from most stories revolving around the horror genre. The compositions were developed thoroughly and consistent attention was paid towards highlighting the subtext of all ideas.'

Alarmingly entertaining

'A superb collection of short stories with a message hidden within each one. The writing style is exquisite, the themes dark and raw.'

BEHAVING BADLY

M. HENNINGHAM

First published in the UK in 2010

Michele Henningham

For my father, go placidly amid the noise and haste...

Opening line of the poem "Desiderata" by Max Ehrmann.

About the Author

M. Henningham is a published author who won the 2014 inaugural Bonnie Greer OBE Stories to Read Aloud Competition. She was also published in What Lies Beneath — A Collection of Short Stories from the Kingston Writing School. Selected by Hilary Mantel and Bonnie Greer, OBE. Michele's writing screenplays and collections of short stories that are thrillers with a twist or two. Kingston University produced 'Off the Page', which features her Unscrupulous Pigs. Michele also took part in a series of workshops at Kingston Writing School and read some of her stories at Kingston University, in the Rose theatre, Ram Jam in Kingston, and the Star of Kings, London. Michele received a highly commended for a short story in Writers' Forum and was long-listed by the Fish Short Story Prize, 2015.

INTRODUCTION

Welcome to a world where each tale is a whisper that beckons you into the depths of the unknown. This enigmatic collection, born from the shadows of inspiration, unveils itself with a series of stories that will leave your senses tingling and your mind craving more. The journey begins with '**Soulless**,' a gripping narrative that follows a young woman's desperate quest to break free from the clutches of a relentless stalker. The inspiration for this tale was drawn from the haunting echoes of real-life stories of resilience and survival. As you venture further into the heart of darkness, '**Delusion 13**' awaits, a thrilling tale that ensnares a luckless man who believes he has discovered the woman of his dreams. Feel the city's pulse in '**Shootin' Candy**,' a talc that dives into the themes of power and greed. This story thrusts a privileged teen past the point of no return, where morality hangs in the balance and the dark side of the tracks beckons. '**Tell Him to Run**' unfolds as a poignant exploration of choices born from desperation and poverty. The inspiration for this tale was ignited by the indomitable spirit of those facing insurmountable odds. '**Behaving Badly**' delves into the psyche of an unstable young man fiercely protective of his parents. This chilling narrative explores the lengths one can go to ensure the safety of those they love. Brace yourself for a journey where the shadows hold secrets that will leave you questioning the boundaries between darkness and light.

Contents

Soulless	11
Delusion 13	21
Shootin' Candy	32
Tell Him to Run	45
Behaving Badly	59
Blackballed	69

Soulless

I squinted through the peephole with my good eye. I saw the front door, bright flashes of light, and a darting shadow. Eyes wide, I held my breath, hoping to catch another glimpse of the shadow, but nothing happened. After covering the peephole, I verified that the door was locked. Turning to walk away, I then turned back to double-check the lock. Only minutes ago, I had been in the kitchen and couldn't remember if I had done it.

As I stood by the door, the tantalising aroma of someone's dinner drifted through the doorjamb. For a moment, it brought me right back to the good old school dinners. I was happy to confirm that it definitely wasn't the notorious boiled cabbage. I closed my eyes and took a few deep breaths to see if I could identify the scent. I'd say it was probably Shepherd's pie, which was proper winter fodder. My stomach rumbled in agreement

I put on the door chain but left out the rubber stop before setting about finding something to eat until Gator returned. He had shot out like a lightning bolt with *my* mobile phone and *my* ride to get a Chinese takeaway, but I didn't know if he had gone up Harrow Road or to China. He was like that sometimes. To say I was starving was an understatement. I would've eaten from the bare hands of a leper, given half a chance. Gator said, 'It's wrong to say starving; you should say you're hungry because children in Africa are starving.'

I found a shrivelled and bruised pomegranate lurking at the back of the fridge. Scoring the skin with a bottle opener, I broke it open. While forcing out the sweet dark arils, I thought about Gator's Africa thing. A few arils flew across the room, and I hunted them down. I found one hiding under the radiator and showed it no mercy. Just like in a game of Monopoly, it didn't pass 'Go' or collect two hundred pounds. Also, I couldn't let it ruin the plush, cream shag pile; they stain. I didn't even consider washing it and popped it straight into my mouth. Gator told me that food was okay to eat as long as I picked it up within five seconds, and that was all right by me.

While I savoured the bittersweetness and the satisfaction of having something in my stomach, it gurgled as if saying thank you. I got so carried away picking up arils and cramming them into my mouth that the juice dripped down my chin. Looking down, I saw purple splotches blossoming on my Pucci dress, which was a sample from Fashion Week.

Suddenly, someone pressed the buzzer. A few seconds later, they pressed it again and again. After a few minutes, it sounded jammed. I attempted to get up, but my hands were too sticky to touch anything.

"Who is it?" I shouted.

No one answered. I muted the TV and listened to the silence, using my tongue to push a small white seed from between my teeth. I giggled to myself, thinking Gator was messing about. He was known for being a goofer - a prankster to all who knew him. Once, at his flat, he hid outside, and when I came out, he jumped up and scared me with one of those scary ghost masks. He gave me a full-blown heart-pounding panic attack and laughed his head off while I struggled to catch my breath. He just stood there, enjoying me being scared witless. At times, I tried to give him a taste of his own medicine, but I couldn't get the timing right, and my pranks would fail miserably and he would find a way to flip them on me.

I heard muffled talking and listened to a voice I didn't expect to hear again, at least not until our date in court. My heart pounded in my ears, and I felt like it would drop right through me to the floor. I licked my dry, sticky lips. How in hell did he find me?
He kept going on at me to open the door and threatened to kick it down when I refused. I prayed he would give up, but that would be too easy. He tried to kick the door down and screamed about how he was going to mess me up. My fingers trembled as I scratched the chronic hives at the top of my back, and he pushed and fiddled with the lock.

"What do you want, Kane?" I asked, raising the plate in my hand.

"Wanna talk, that's—" he said, working the lock.

"T-there's nothing to talk about. I'm going out. My friend will be here any minute."

"That's cool, Mani. Give me a few minutes, and I promise I'll go. I miss my boo," he said and pushed against the door. The wood strained, and I was sure he'd get in.

"Kane, you're not even meant to be here. If they find out."

"Come on, Mani," he interrupted, "just two minutes, please. I beg."

"How did you get in anyway?"

"Told them upstairs my fiancée was pregnant and not answering the phone," he sniggered.

I knew I had good reason to hate my neighbors. The first time I saw the flat, I needed to pee but waited ages for anyone to let me in. Kane gave up picking the lock and put his shoulder to the door. It was just a matter of time before he'd break it down and get inside. Then, I'd have to explain what happened to the landlord and find money to repair the damages. My hands shook like nobody's business as I put the plate on the floor. Some arils and juice slid onto the carpet. I turned over onto my knees before standing. Picking up the plate with one hand, I licked my fingers on the other and wiped them on my leggings. My heart hammered while Kane worked on the lock.

Whimpering like a puppy, I looked around for something — anything to use. I'd never heard of anyone getting arrested for GBH with a bottle opener or soggy pomegranate skin. Bracing my shoulders, I held onto the door handle. At that point, sweat popped out on my face like grease bubbles, and I found it difficult to breathe.

"OK. OK. I'll come out. We'll talk."

My manicured fingernails clicked as I struggled to release the door chain. My hands shook so much that a tip got caught and flew off with a chunk of nail. Cursing, I opened the door, and it flew back in my face, bouncing against the wall. Pomegranate arils exploded into the air, making quite a spectacle. The plate slammed into my face before crashing against the skirting board. Kane burst through the door.

"Get out!" I backed away from him, squishing arils underfoot.

"Not until I'm finished with you, sweetheart."

"Leave me alone, for God's sake!" I ran to the corner of the living room by the window, which was as far away as I could get.

"Seriously, Kane, my friend will be here any minute. We're going out!" Pursing my lips to stop the trembling, I pressed myself into the corner.

"Oh, so you've got a friend now, have you? Don't you mean my best mate, Gator? He's like blood to me! Didn't take you guys long, huh?"

"We're just friends, honest."

"Wasn't I enough for you?"

Kane rested both hands on the wall on either side of my head. He looked down at me with cold hazel eyes.

"Look, I... It's not that. We had finished."

"No, you binned me." He pointed his big finger in my face, and his spit hit me like a loaded paintbrush.

"Look, let's try again... it doesn't have to be over," I begged, reaching up to hold his hands. I wondered if he heard the lie in my voice.

He turned away from me.

"It's too late for that."

He continued to vent with his back to me, his hands dancing all over the place.

"Aww, hon," I said, reaching out to him again, "it's not too late for us. We can fix this, get it right... try again."

"Shut it," he said, brushing me off.

I looked up at him while he glared with soulless eyes. If he could have chewed me up and spat me out, he would have. A phone rang upstairs. A woman yelled, 'I got it!' It stopped ringing. Someone entered the house, climbed the stairs, and disappeared into a flat. The theme tune for a popular gameshow blared. Kane pulled me so close and pressed his body into mine. I gasped as he pushed his tongue into my mouth. It might as well have been a diamond-tipped drill boring into molten rock. His breath stank something rotten. I'd guess a mix of hunger and pure hatred. I felt his growing excitement as he forced thick, muscular thighs between my legs. In the earlier days, it used to turn me on, but I was disgusted. Absolutely disgusted that I ever let him get that close. This was the monster that had once given me pleasure I couldn't give myself. I tried to move my head as Kane moaned with one hand in his pocket. I edged away and wiped my chin with the back of my hand.

Out of nowhere, a honking horn shattered the silence. I shot to the window to see if it was Gator. Pressing my face up against the glass, the coolness was so refreshing. As the glass misted over in a wide white arc, I forced down a lump in my throat because it wasn't him. A few seconds later, Kane shoved my face into the glass and ground against me. He squeezed my breasts like stress balls. I peeled his fingers off and stumbled to get away. As I turned, I saw his hulking silhouette blocking the doorway. Damn, he was quick and far bigger than I remembered. I backed into the corner. Kane came after me again and ran his fingers through my hair. I remembered how he used to slice off bits of skin on his fingers with a Stanley knife. I closed my eyes and winced as my hair caught on jagged bits. Kane looked down and smiled at me, as you would at a child who's written their name for the first time.

"Still beautiful, eh?" he said, toying with my hair.

"Don't, Kane, please don't!"

"I wonder what you'd look like without. Have you heard about a woman's glory?"

I took a deep breath and forced my head down out of his reach. His mobile phone rang, so he swore and flipped it open, answering as if it were just another day in the office. Again, I scooted to the window. The only thing trying to get in was the streetlamp's orangey glow and penny-sized raindrops. I watched as they punished the window pane. My landline phone lay disconnected on the floor. What could I do? Kane put away his mobile phone and pulled out a zombie knife. He smacked the blade against his palm as he came towards me, then started jabbing at me like he was some kind of Zorro, so I backed into the corridor. I managed to dodge him until I ended up in the bedroom. I fell over my suitcase, and something metallic scratched my calf. It was the padlock. Kane looked over and smiled like a demon. The diamond stud in his front tooth glinted in the dim light. I struggled to my feet, but he swung a right hook. I didn't just see the odd star but pure constellations as I slid down the back of the wardrobe.

"Kane, why the hell?" I shouted, struggling to get out.

"Because I can," he smirked and wiped the sweat from his brow. All of a sudden, something snapped in my head. A rush of blood surged around my body, and my temples throbbed. Kane giggled as I leapt and clawed his face and neck, drawing blood.

"Look, Kane, please stop. It's done. It's finished!"

"Well, I'm not done yet, Mani."

He stormed from the room, rushing into the bathroom. After pulling on the light switch, he grunted a couple of times before he swore like a trooper. I guessed that it was because he didn't like what he saw in the mirror. After all these years, he didn't think I had it in me, so he hadn't seen it coming. He had taken my kindness and easygoing nature for weakness. Kane stomped back into the room with a pair of my 40 denier tights draped around his neck.

He shut the door and forced me face down on the bed. Then, he straddled me, grabbed my wrists, and tied them with my tights. I screamed and swore as much as the pillow allowed, and like a bull that's impossible to ride, I tried to buck him. I really tried.

"Please stop, Kane, you're hurting me."

"Yeah, Mani, and what'll you do if I don't, huh – get Gator?"

He bent over and pulled my neck back with a fistful of my hair.

"You keep thinking he's coming to save you, bitch. Newsflash."

"What — what do you mean?"

"Let's say he's no longer an issue."

"What have you done?"

"Wouldn't you like to know?"

My spine clicked as he flipped me over onto my back. He pulled my leggings and thong down, whipped them off, and threw them on the floor. In the other hand, he held the knife that freed the remaining buttons on my dress. They ricocheted off the radiator and walls and flew everywhere. Kane cut and hauled the dress off and chucked it over his shoulder. Yanking up my bra, he gnawed on sweat-soaked breasts. A few minutes later, he stopped as if in deep thought and darted out of the bedroom and into the living room. The sudden chill on my chest made me shiver as the sweat and saliva dried. A gut-wrenching sob rose from somewhere deep inside me, and I yearned for him to go.

In minutes, I heard his growing frustration as things crashed to the floor. A brief silence was followed by the flick of a light switch and the creak of bedsprings coming from upstairs. Kane rifled through my jewellery box, but I didn't care. He could have what he wanted as long as he left me alone. A heavy silence told me he'd found something when he stomped back into the corridor.

The door chain jangled, and I breathed a sigh of relief when the door opened and closed. I wondered if he'd really gone. But I didn't know how gone gone was. No one knew me to be religious, but I thanked God. Minutes later, my shoulders relaxed, and with each sob, the tension drained away.

But after a while, Kane sniggered and marched down the corridor, shouting that he was ready. For what? My heart played African war drums because Kane had looped the door chain and put on the padlock. A scraping sound filled the air as he rubbed his hands together at the bedside. Like a swimmer on Hampstead Heath in the heart of winter, he quickly undressed and got into bed with me. First, he undid the bonds and re-tied my hands so they were in front. Then he raised them over my head, stopped laughing, licked the side of my face, and whispered, "This time, I'll finish you properly."

Kane moaned as his thick, muscular thighs forced my legs apart. Throughout, I struggled and screamed until hoarse as a hot thickness bored into me. My knees braced, but I soon tired. Beads of his sweat dripped and burned my eyes. I shut them real tight and lay there and let him. My nose tingled at the hot, oniony aroma mixed with stale cologne. Somewhere, a siren blared and faded into the distance. For all the noise, not one soul came. Kane snorted and laughed in his sleep. Was he dreaming? About me? About what he'd done to me? The bastard was thoroughly contented in my bed. If he had been a decent human being, this might have been an ideal scenario, and we could've made it all the way to life's finish line, but no. That was too easy for Kane.

I searched the darkness for the neon alarm clock. It was just gone quarter past three. My body pressed into the sodden sheets as burning tears rolled down my face. Kane slept with his hands under his head as if tanning on the Costa del Sol. I hated him with every ounce of blood I had left. The hours flew by like a clock on fast-forward, but still, no one came. The birds chirped even before the morning light came into the room. Thinking about escaping made my heart pound so loudly that I half-expected it to rouse him. I prayed it wouldn't wake him up. Keeping an eye on him, I lowered my arms. I tasted blood on my lips, and sweat gathered like a moustache on my upper lip. I tested the knots on my bonds, figuring out how to untie them and get away. In the darkness, I searched the room for something sharp. As I pulled my wrists apart, the idea of using scissors struck me.

Kane shifted a little in his sleep. Holding my breath, I kept my eyes on his face, waiting for any sign of waking up. Silently getting out of bed, I swung my legs over the edge. Attempting to stand, my legs felt wobbly, so I clung to the bed and shuffled around its perimeter. Reaching the dresser, I cautiously opened the top drawer using just my fingers. With a nail, I pried out the scissors, trying not to make a sound.

Sitting in a quiet corner, I was puzzled over how to cut the tights. The angles were tricky, making it more complicated than I thought. Adjusting my grip, I brought the scissors back towards myself, determined to be free. The room was silent except for the muffled sounds of my efforts. After the struggle, my wrists bore the evidence of my escape attempt – a few drops of blood as I moved stealthily around the bed, searching for Kane's clothes. A muttered curse escaped my lips as my toe collided with the unforgiving bed frame. The sudden noise startled Kane, who promptly sat up and reached over to switch on the lamp, the light revealing a mixture of confusion and alertness in his eyes.

"Going somewhere?"

He shot out of bed and punched me in the stomach.

"Please leave me the fuck alone," I wheezed, clutched my stomach, and dropped to my knees. His knife glistened under the foot of the bed. I crawled to get it, straightened up, and turned to face him.

"Go on, Miss Goody-Goody! You ain't got the guts."

I jabbed, but Kane grabbed my wrist, and we rolled, at first, him on top, then me, back and forth, arms and legs laced.

Kicking him between the legs, I rushed to the corner. As I stooped, something sharp and sour trickled from between my legs.

The knife stuck out from under a box. We both rushed to get it, but I got there first. I held the knife up just as he charged. I lunged, and the blade crunched into his broad, muscular chest. For a moment, it was as if time stood still. It was so quiet that you could have heard a mouse sneeze.

"Straight to dust, fucker! All you had to do was leave me the fuck alone!"

Kane's eyes opened wide, first with shock, then with what looked like terror. He gulped, struggling for breath. As he reached for the knife, blood splashed over his hands and splattered on the wall. He crumpled to the floor in slow motion, and a soft groan parted his lips. I touched him and heard a muted moan. There was a look in his eyes. He looked surprised. I think it was surprise. Was he trying to say something?

"Oh God, Kane. Please, please, please. Oh, please, Kane. You can't die on me. You can't."

I checked for a pulse in his neck before his wrist. Stressed to the max, I didn't know if what I felt was his or mine. Again, I pressed my fingers to his neck and waited. Kane twitched once, but other than that, nothing. Exhausted, I leaned against the wall. My tongue felt alien, like a foreigner in a strange land, as it travelled over swollen and cracked lips. I tasted salt. My nose ran, a welcome change from the metallic taste of blood. Giddy with adrenaline, I gazed down at the soulless piece of shit that blighted my life. Moving silently around him, I located his trousers and grabbed the padlock key. Pulling on the remnants of my dress, I slipped out. I had to make my getaway before he woke – if he did – given his reputation for keeping promises.

Delusion 13

From the moment I saw her, I knew she was the one—no doubt about it. She was the bee's knees, and I felt it deep down in my bones. There was just something about her that captivated me. Racing downstairs to catch the 17:57 before the doors closed, I couldn't help but notice how the sun kissed her face. It might sound cheesy, but she was next-level gorgeous if that was even a thing. Miraculously, I made it to the bottom without tearing my eyes away or crashing headfirst to the ground. Her skin had a warm caramel hue, and I guessed she had a mix of African and Asian ancestry. Her thick, dark hair bounced around her shoulders, complementing her sparkling almond eyes, which were blacker than black. As I regained my senses and stopped drooling, the train pulled out.

As days and weeks passed, thoughts of her consumed my mind. She was the first thing I thought of every morning and the last before sleep. I daydreamed about spending every waking moment with her and imagined the adventures we could share.

Just back from a not-so-memorable date, I sought solace at Neon Nites with a glass of 'forgetting juice.' Suddenly, the door burst open, and there she was, strutting in as if she owned the place—remarkable and perfect. All eyes were fixated on her, irrespective of their relationship status. My heart threatened to explode in my chest. She exuded freedom and a boldness that stirred most men. From the stereo, a loud, peculiar Oriental beat filled the room. As I supped my pint, I watched her swaying in the middle of the room with her eyes closed. Something lurched in my gut—a strange mix of fear and excitement, a feeling entirely new to me.

Audacious as ever, Mark asked her for a dance, but she blanked him. It rarely happened with other girls, but she had me soft. Completely saft. Alf sensed I was losing shape.

"Wakey, cakey, gym rat."

"What?"

"Hope you got life insurance."

"What you on?"

"Spicy, that one."

"Oi, give it a rest. I'm Willy the Conqueror," I said as he carried on filling my head with tales of the unexpected about her—how she'd married, but they always rowed and made up. Her husband, a jailbird, frequently called it quits as her wild ways tested his patience. There was lots of shouting, and rumour had it they often exchanged blows. Police were known to frequent their doorstep. One night, they dragged the husband out, kicking, screaming, and bloodied as if he had been hauled through prickers. She always claimed self-defense but wanted him back. However, when the police investigated, they ran a check, arrested, and detained him for a previous case. She divorced him in a heartbeat. When Alf wiped his brow and took a breath, I looked over, and something inside me craved her even more. Then, after a silent exchange of glances, she approached and sat beside me.

"Fancy a bevvy?" I said, acting unfazed.

"You offering?"

"Mm-hmm."

"The name's Ninako."

"John, a pleasure," I said, trying to keep calm.

I couldn't think of anything else that didn't sound too corny, and that seemed to get things going. I stared as she tapped stiletto fingernails on the bar in time to the music. Glancing around, I realised that everyone in the bar was staring at her, no, us, so I straightened my back and stuck my pigeon chest out. I mean, I had no money to speak of, but I felt rich as if I were related to the Rockefeller family. I had never had a girl make me feel that way before.

Ninako reached over to shake my hand. I wiped my palm on my jeans before extending it, then quickly pulled it back. I thought it might still be clammy and didn't want to share that. While Alf prepared our drinks, Ninako excused herself and sashayed through the saloon doors to the ladies' room. However, she stopped and held the door ajar. Slowly turning, she fixed me with a pouting expression. Heat rushed to my cheeks, and I found myself unable to look away, trapped by the intensity of her gaze. Alf brought our drinks over.

"Oi, oi, John," he said, "them ain't ya type... ain't ya, reg, mate."

I grinned. "Whatever, Alf."

"Shout if ya need protectin'," he said, shaking his head from side to side.

"Check out the guns," I said, flexing my puny biceps.

"You'll be needin' a real one... she'll eat ya right up," he said in a low voice. "Call me when ya just a bag of bones."

He set our drinks on napkins in front of me. "Bones," he said, "she'll grind ya up and spit ya out!"

"Nudge, nudge... wink, wink, Alf."

Alf started singing, "Hey, John, oh, John, if you will. Please send a dear Johnny for her to thrill."

"Okay... all right," I said, wishing he'd cut it out. I'd twisted bits of tissue until there were loads of rolled-up balls on the bar.

"Out while ya can. Y'hear?" Alf said, "Now! Before it gets too deep for ya, and ya drown in ya own ketchup!"

But when Ninako returned, his words meant zip. She'd powdered her face and was all lipstick fresh. I passed her a drink, and we clinked glasses. She downed it straight, leaned over, and planted one on my cheek. A grin crept across my face as I sat bathing in her glow. Minutes later, Ninako pushed her glass forward for another drink. She was quiet for a minute before moving closer to me, putting her lips close to my ear, "I've only got one thing to ask you."

"W-what?"

"You like fire?" she murmured with a Cheshire cat gleam in her eyes.

I didn't know where to look as another hot blush crept up my neck.

Before I knew it, it was three in the morning. We were poggled but not ready to call it a night. As Alf started shutting down the lights, a teenager badgered him about giving water to children in Tigray. Ninako wanted to have coffee at my place, so we left the car and took an Uber. Upon arrival, I shot into the kitchen and drummed my fingers on the counter while waiting for the kettle to boil. After making the coffee, I brought the cups in and found Ninako sprawled out on the sofa, her eyes focused on the television screen that wasn't even on. She looked as if she were miles away. Holding her cup and saucer, I sat down beside her. She peered at the gap between us.

"You're not scared, are you?" She took the cup and saucer from me, placing it on the table.

I gazed into my cup for a moment, then replied, "Who, me?"

"You wanna?" she said, tugging at a bra strap, revealing a full breast.

"Does a bear—?" I said, putting my cup and saucer on the table.

"It's getting... so... cold," she said, tweaking a nipple.

"What about coffee?"

"You've got more, right?"

"B-but..." I said, nodding.

Ninako reached for her cup, but I passed it to her. We drank the coffee in a silence so thick you could cut it with a knife. Afterwards, I gave her the grand tour. Minutes later, she kicked off her shoes and rushed into the bathroom. I checked my teeth in the kitchen mirror before dimming the lights. I didn't know if I should shower, shit, or shave. While I was going through a minor breakdown, Ninako loomed in the doorway, exuding pure seduction. In no time, we explored bases before crashing into the bedroom and collapsing onto the bed. With lightning speed, I struggled out of my keks, then stood and watched as Ninako opened and closed at the knees. I got on top of her, experiencing a level of smoothness and tightness like never before. Pulling her close, I started in on the breasts. I sampled one like a fine black truffle before moving to the other, savouring every moment.

I knew that if I rushed, it would be over before it started, so I paced myself and took it real slow.

I swear to no head-scratching; I had never been lucky enough to meet a woman who moved like her. There was no lying and thinking of England. She really knew how to bring the heat, if you catch my drift. Ninako was a rare breed, showcasing her skills before ending with the reverse cowgirl, which was not the most woman-friendly position in the world. I was knocked out! However, two hours later, I woke up to find her staring blankly at the ceiling. Propping myself up on my elbow, it seemed like she didn't even notice me or know why she was in my bed. To be honest, the look in her eyes freaked me right out. I thought about it for a long time and couldn't get back to sleep.

In the afternoon, we lounged in bed, and she shared stories about her ex-husband—the punk. As she opened up, I couldn't help but feel a deep sympathy for her. Later, I reflected on him, vowing that he wouldn't get another chance to hurt my woman as long as I lived. Ninako nestled in the crook of my arm for the longest time, and it felt right. It felt good. It felt like she was meant to be there. Later that night, I didn't want her to leave - ever, but she told me she had some urgent things to do.

Now, because I was very close to my parents, I shared almost everything with them. Excited to share my good news, I called and told them I'd met someone, someone I felt was on my level and someone I thought was for keeps. Initially, they seemed happy for me, but when I mentioned Ninako's marriage, it crushed me when they warned me off. My mum kept bringing up some old-school girlfriend who still lived in the neighbourhood while my dad tried to sway me with money. They even invited me away for the weekend to talk me out of it, but their efforts failed. For once, I decided to prove them wrong, hoping they'd come around when they saw how happy we were.

Months passed, and to be honest, things were off the charts. Everyone heard about fifty shades of grey, but Ninako tipped the scale at fifty-thousand shades of vermillion. What red-blooded man didn't want that? She had zero inhibitions and always knew how to push the envelope, test the limits, or stretch the boundaries, whatever you want to call it.

We became so tight that she wanted to dive into the marriage thing again. I suggested there was no hurry and that we should wait awhile. Unaware I was watching, something dark flashed in her eyes when sheer frustration gripped her by the throat. Ninako was relentless. After a few months, she wore me down, and I eventually surrendered. She gazed at me silently, then wrapped her arms around my neck, pulled me close, and kissed my forehead.

"Oh, John, you're the best. You mean it?"

"Promise," I said. "Let's." I gazed at her, mesmerised by her expression.

"We'll be together, always," she beamed at me. "And perhaps 'til death.

So, we had a quiet marriage. It was a low-key affair because my parents refused to come. After the wedding, there were many times when Ninako was like a red rag to a bull for the slightest thing, but I overlooked it. I would do anything for peace.

Alone, I went to my parents for their anniversary. Mum was gauging our temperature and asked if everything was all right between us. Forcing a smile, I assured her that things were great. When I returned home that night and washed up for bed, Ninako sobbed about wanting someone to love. I mean, she had me, for Christ's sake, and I was doubtful about having children. I just wasn't sure because my parents' voices kept drilling into my drums. Exhausted from overthinking, I fell asleep, only to wake up with Ninako on top, riding me like a jockey at The Kentucky Derby. My heart pounded, and sweat drenched my forehead. Breathing heavily, I shoved her and turned over. It took a while before the night air dried the sweat that soaked me. Weeks later, she came in all Colgate mode, telling me we would be parents.

My one crumb of comfort, Evie, came into the world. Nothing was too much for my pride and joy. One Saturday afternoon, I took her shopping in town and let her pick out her shoes. They were pink, sparkly things with lights and lace. The first time she wore them, Ninako fought her because at bedtime, Evie wouldn't take them off. Sweating, Ninako freed one while Evie screamed blue murder. It tore me apart.

I rushed over and wedged between them, telling Ninako to wait until she slept.

Anyway, I had to keep it together for Evie's sake. I worked hard and late to ensure she lacked nothing. Sometimes, Ninako called me at work and bombarded me with irrelevant questions. Initially, my colleagues found it amusing, so I laughed it off, too. However, things became stranger than fiction. When I got home—I didn't tell them—she would close the bedroom door to get handy with me. Soon, Evie became my sole reason to go home, but I dreaded Ninako's wrath. I often stayed later at work, then went to the pub to lather up before facing her.

Wagging tongues made their way back to Alf. So, one night, when I turned up sporting two black eyes, I tried some lame excuse about rugby, but Alf knew better. He reached under the counter and slid a handgun over the bar. I clutched it in my armpit before tucking it into the waistband of my slacks. Sneaking into the house when I thought Ninako would be asleep, I slithered into bed like a mouse sucking on ice.

That night, I meant to lock it in the bedside cabinet but drifted off with it under my pillow. I remembered to lock it away as I heard Ninako making breakfast in the morning. However, Ninako started a pointless row, setting Evie off crying. Eventually, I had to go to work, but I worried about leaving Evie with Ninako. Even on my days off, I fretted about Evie being around her. As I left the house sometimes, Evie cried and stamped her feet. Ninako would pick her up, grip and pat her back like a drum, all while grinning over her shoulder. Something about that grin made me feel uneasy.

One afternoon, I was watching England play Brazil in the World Cup. It was a heated game, and you could feel the tension in the air. The players were giving it their all on the field. Every kick, every save felt like a mini heart attack. The anticipation hung thick as England tried to break through Brazil's defence, and the excitement was contagious. During half-time, I was heading to the kitchen for another beer. Ninako, preoccupied with Evie in the dining room, hadn't seen me. I watched as she fed Evie in her high chair.

Evie didn't like greens, and we'd already discussed the force-feeding issue. My empty bottle crashed to the floor when Evie's eyes rolled, and she gagged while attempting to swallow. I completely lost it when it came through her nostrils. A red mist enveloped me, and I didn't even feel the glass needles pricking my feet as I propelled Ninako across the room. Evie gave a loud, heart-breaking wail, reaching out her hands for me to pick her up. I scooped her up in my arms and showered her with kisses in the living room.

Later that night, it took a while to settle Evie for bed. I read bedtime stories, sang a few of her favourite nursery rhymes, and she eventually drifted off. After leaving Evie's room, I found Ninako curled up on her side, sobbing. I tried to soothe her until she relaxed, but our conversation and my stress led me to accidentally mention the D-word. There was never a right time to mention the D-word. Ninako's face changed; her eyes narrowed into slits, and her lips curled into an expression I hadn't seen before. She lay motionless, staring into the dark. I rubbed her back, but she grunted and shrugged me off.

Ninako plunged deeper and deeper into the bottle. The doctor prescribed something for anxiety and stress, warning her to stay off alcohol and advising her to schedule another assessment. Ninako took the prescription but ignored subsequent assessment appointments. I mean, sometimes I drank liquor like I was thirsty, but she did too and double-dosed on medication. Soon, Ninako became a powder keg rolling downhill fast. She was drinking, drugging and hanging with the wrong crowd. Ninako stayed out for days at a time, and no one knew where until Alf mentioned he'd seen her with her jailbird ex-husband.

After finalising the divorce, I gained sole custody of Evie, and we moved. Ninako was none too pleased, given she only had supervised visits. Well, she blew up and stalked me—no, us. On a Monday evening, as I came out of work, I was just about to get into the Jeep when she and the jailbird jumped me. They wrestled me to the ground and tore me up as I curled into a ball. My uncontrollable shakes weren't as bad when they arrested and put her in a psychiatric unit for observation, but the jailbird escaped.

For the first in a long while, I slept a little more through the night. However, in the days that followed, the flutters in my stomach turned to nausea. One night, there was a creaking sound near the bed. I sat up straight, but all I saw was total darkness. I thought Ninako had come back. Even after putting Evie to bed, I kept getting up to ensure I had locked the doors. On my way back to bed, I checked on her, ventured into the living room, and peered out of the window into the blackness. The following week, we stayed with my parents. It felt like Chinese water torture with the way they kept asking me the same old questions I had no answers for, so by the weekend, I'd had enough of them, too.

Squinting in the warm September sunshine, I picked up Evie from the child-minder to attend Max's birthday party. As we approached the house, I glanced down at her, beaming from ear to ear, skipping along at my side. She had her pink magic shoes on and didn't even glance over her shoulder at me as she walked off with Debbie. I climbed into the Jeep and smiled; my little princess was growing up. Before heading to the pub for footy highlights and a few pints with the lads, I made a quick stop at the supermarket.

When I returned home, the front door knocker seemed... wonky. Could it have been the postman? Did they knock so hard that they dislodged it? My tongue lolled in my mouth like a pebble because something told me it wasn't the postman. Peering through the window, there was nothing unusual about the living room. It was empty. But I still couldn't bring myself to go inside and put the shopping away, so I returned to the Jeep and called Mum. I heard the tremor of nerves in her voice as she told me to relax and go back to the pub for safety in numbers or something like that. So, I did. After a few rounds, we had moved on to football songs and chants when a newsflash came on:

'An armed man, masquerading as a guard, assisted three women in escaping from a mental institution, resulting in the deaths of two guards. Police apprehended two of the women, found roaming in the countryside, but the man and the third were still at large.'

I remembered the knocker. Shooting to my feet, I slammed the glass on the table and rushed home. Frantic sweat broke out all over my body when I saw glass shards covering the ground by the side door. The bedroom window latch hung loose, and the curtain fluttered in the open window. Mouth open in shock, I flew upstairs —two at a time—and stumbled into my bedroom. My stuff was all over the floor in pure chaos. I opened the bedside cabinet. Empty. While standing there, my mobile phone vibrated. When I put it to my ear, there was a crackling sound, then silence. I dropped the phone on the bed. Seconds later, it rang again; I was about to lose it when I recognised Debbie's voice. She asked what time I planned to pick up Evie. With a sigh of relief, I told her I'd be there at 7 pm on the dot, which gave me about forty-five minutes. Just before ending the call, I emphasised not to let Evie go with *anyone* else. In a blind panic, I tossed everything everywhere but couldn't remember where I had put the car keys.

After a few minutes, I found the spares and jumped in the Jeep. I fired up the engine, but it didn't start straight away. I gunned it again, and it revved up, spouting lots of smoke. I tore out of the drive and hit the main road. As I shot through the next junction, the lights changed, but I kept going, not seeing the police car. The siren blared, and I saw them in the rear-view mirror, urging me to pull over. I pulled in and punched the steering wheel.

"Shit!"

"Put your hands where we can see them!"

A police officer got out of the car and approached my window, instructing me to cut the engine and step out. I tried to explain about Evie, lost keys, and forgotten papers. The other officer joined when he saw his colleague struggling. They sprawled me across the front of their patrol car while they explored the Jeep, checked my pockets, and radioed my details. As I waited, the sun was fast disappearing, my heart pounded, and sweat poured. Frustration built up because 7 pm had come and gone long ago. Determined to get Evie, I made a run for it, hoping to explain later. However, an officer anticipated my move and grabbed me.

"Look, sir, if you stay calm—"

"I have to pick up Evie, my daughter. *Now*!"

"What's your name and address?" The other officer got out his walkie-talkie and asked for information about ownership of the Jeep. Again, I pulled away and tried to get into the Jeep, but an officer caught me and spun me around. They both slammed on top of me, cuffing and reading my rights.

"We believe you've escaped," the other officer said and dragged me into the back of the patrol car while they ran checks.

The sky had darkened by the time they released me. They kept on apologising and brushing me down. Running more than late, I arrived at Debbie's. Filled with joy, she rushed out, talking about how much Evie loved the clowns and magic and didn't want to leave.

"What do you mean, didn't want to leave?" I exclaimed, throwing my hands up to the sky. "But I told you!"

"Well, Ninako insisted she was Evie's mother... and that you asked her to get Evie as you were running late."

"Oh. Shit! She's crazy! Why? Which way did she go?" I shouted, looking around.

Debbie's eyes widened with fear. She pointed at the gutter. My gaze followed the direction of her finger. Her face dropped. There, covered in dirt with its pink lights flashing, lay one of Evie's magic shoes. My chest hurt. I couldn't catch my breath.

Shootin' Candy

I must not do lines in the toilets
I must not do lines in the toilets
I must not do lines in the toilets

They kicked Bastian out for doing lines but not the written variety. He moved his belongings from the halls and into a studio in Maida Vale. Bastian drifted through a string of jobs that never lasted, as he despised taking orders. He almost lost his mind searching for meaningful things to do.

Soon, he drifted around Ladbroke Grove, seeking action. Little did he know that his luck would lead him on a journey of no return. Bored as a clock with no hands, he wandered until he encountered White Boy Gator, sampled his wares, and quickly transformed into a shotter. Bastian delivered coke wraps to the Savile Row suits, who preferred him over the likes of White Boy Gator. It was an easy gig, but he broke the cardinal rule. For every one or two wraps sold, he smoked or snorted three or four. And it wasn't from profit. That's how the debt spiralled out of control. White Boy Gator warned him to settle up, so every Friday night, they convened on the corner of Sussex Gardens and Edgware Road. Initially, the meetings yielded success, and Bastian managed to make small, steady payments. Unfortunately, this was short-lived. He fell on even harder times as he had used more. Additionally, Bastian owed rent, and his parents had given up attempting to save him from himself. He couldn't even afford the air he breathed, but White Boy Gator wasn't in the mood to hear any of it.

"Right, same time tomorrow. I'm coming for you. You'd better sort me out," he spat over his shoulder as he jumped into a white Escalade. Then, he barrelled through traffic, almost wiping out a grain-sized woman and a dog, like a rat on a string. Bastian watched until the van disappeared, shrugged, and jammed his hands deep into his jeans pockets. But if he had known how wide the gates of hell were about to open, he might have given his situation a little more care and attention. Although the cold sweat formed and sat like a thin moustache over his top lip, he neither noticed nor cared. The relentless craving beckoned with unbridled intensity, making White Boy Gator the least of Bastian's problems. Tomorrow would have to take care of itself, he thought.

"Need to score," he said to himself as he searched through lint balls in his pocket, hoping to find a morsel of cocaine. When he thought he had found something, he almost laughed aloud. But finding nothing, he stooped, wiped the sweat from his brow with his hand, then used his fingers to slick his quiff in a black Mercedes CLK's wing mirror.

As he straightened up, he noticed pigeons pecking at a puddle of vomit near the front wheel. Among them was an albino one that hopped on a broken leg, all scabby with bald patches. It reminded him of White Boy Gator, minus the dreadlocks. For a moment, he yearned to wring its scrawny neck, grind the bones until they turned to powder, and snort them. However, that's not what held his attention. What made him zoom in looked like money sticking out of the muck. It had a reddish hue, possibly a fifty-pound note. His heart did a triple-salchow. He scratched his right temple and crouched for a better look. A Ford Mondeo pulled up beside the CLK. The stocky, bald man wound down the window and curled his index finger towards Bastian.

"What do you want?" Bastian said before the driver could speak.

"Haven't we had the pleasure?" said the driver, poking his head out of the window.

"Nah, don't think so; you got me mixed up with someone else," Bastian said, rising to stand.

"I never forget a face, me. I remember tryin' to talk to ya, but you was busy servin' drinks at that albino's party. Can't for the life of me remember 'is name. Gator or something."

"Whatever," Bastian said, dismissing him but still thinking about his potential windfall tucked in the chunder on the pavement. The driver nodded and smiled as if remembering. Bastian shivered and ran his fingers through his quiff as the driver's hungry eyes scanned his body. He gazed into Bastian's ice-grey eyes, then slid past his chest before lingering on his crotch. The driver sized him up like a ravenous blackbird about to chow down on a big, fat earthworm. Bastian shifted from one foot to the other as the driver continued to pan down to his Converse-clad feet.

"Fancy a drink?" the driver said, reaching for his wallet.

"Do one, you pervert!"

Bastian waved the man away in disgust. He had done many things for money, but he had not lost the bearings of his moral compass. Scowling, the driver revved the engine and sped off. Bastian bent over to check his good fortune. Plucking it with his fingertips, he shook open the gunk-covered folds before realising it was a magazine cutting. With a dismissive gesture, he tossed it back into the slush, wiped his fingers on his jeans, and sloped off.

The following day, the pounding on the front door roused him from a late night of freeloading. He woke with a jump and sat up in bed, listening. Running his fingers through his quiff, he heard a voice through the letterbox.

"Oi, Bastian, open up," said the voice.

It was White Boy Gator, as promised. He bellowed like a maniac and banged on the windows with the side of his fist. Bastian hid behind the bedroom door, praying White Boy Gator would give up the ghost and leave. However, the noise increased, and it was only a matter of time before the neighbours would call the police. They weren't fond of people who looked like White Boy Gator, causing a ruckus in such an affluent neighbourhood. Bastian rubbed his face to clear the sleep and combed his quiff with his fingers.

A moment of silence followed, and then, to his horror, he heard a scraping sound in the lock. Bastian shot out of the bedroom and slowly opened the front door. White Boy Gator barged in, spitting feathers. The door bashed against the wall hard enough for the handle to leave a dent. White Boy Gator slammed the door shut and attacked Bastian with a barrage of punches. He had no time to react as White Boy Gator smashed him onto the polished parquet floor and shoved his knee into his throat.

"Don't play," White Boy Gator snarled as his thick arms rained down with blows.

"I'm not. I swear."

"Don't think you can mess with my money and get away with it." For a few seconds, White Boy Gator stopped and stared at him, his bulbous eyes bloodshot.

"OK, OK, I'll go... I'll see what's in the bedroom."

White Boy Gator dragged Bastian to his feet and watched him stagger into the bedroom. Bastian closed the door, being careful not to make a sound. He took a few tentative steps, looked over his shoulder, and then stopped, thinking he heard White Boy Gator. Then Bastian tiptoed to the window. At that moment, White Boy Gator's phone rang, and then the air filled with his explosive cackle. Bastian leaned against the wall by the window for a moment to steel his nerves, his heart pounding like someone playing talking drums. With shaky hands and clammy fingers, he lifted the window hooks. The veins pulsed in his trembling arms as he pushed open the window as quietly and as far as it would go. Before easing a knee, then his body, onto the ledge, he glanced at the grass below the window. But in a matter of minutes, a sudden breeze gushed down the middle of his back. Flat on the ledge, Bastian was jerked by the ankles as if a wheelbarrow with an errant wheel. He clutched at the ledge with his fingertips to save himself, but it was no use. He saw the pattern in the wood rushing to meet his face just before his ribs smacked the floor. Stunned, he whimpered as he turned to anticipate White Boy Gator's next move.

"Where's my money?" White Boy Gator punched his left palm with his right fist as he crouched to study Bastian. Rusty blonde dreads hung on his contorted face.

"You'll get it. I swear!" All the spit in Bastian's mouth disappeared, leaving it dry and bitter.

He gasped as White Boy Gator stood and jerked him to his knees.

"I haven't got it... but I'll get it for you... honest," said Bastian, clenching his hands, his knuckles a bright white.

"You better, for real, or you're gonna have to work it off the hard way."

The doorbell rang.

"Bastian, Bastian, are you in there?!" said a posh English voice. They both froze. White Boy Gator shot out through the back door. Bastian realised two things. The first was that it was his landlord, and the second was that White Boy Gator hadn't finished with him. It wasn't over. It would only end when he repaid the debt or was dead.

Bastian slumped against the wall in the corner and listened to the letterbox open and close. He held his breath, waiting for his landlord's footsteps to fade. They were slow at first, then resumed a quicker pace. Bastian peeped through the letterbox. The landlord took a last glance before walking down the road. After a few minutes, Bastian fought back hot, salty tears, but they triumphed, cascading down his cheeks onto his already damp t-shirt. He crawled into the bedroom, lay in the bed beneath the covers, and sobbed.

Sometime later, he summoned the energy and dragged his aching body from the bedroom to the doormat. He sat with his back against the front door, gazing down at a white envelope. Trembling, he reached for it, and his hands shook as he ripped it open, harbouring a strange hope that it contained money. When he realised there was none, he trembled even more.

Staring at the capitals on the eviction notice, it was obvious his savings had vanished, and he'd sold everything he owned. A throbbing ache in the pit of his stomach told him things would get far worse before they got better.

In sheer frustration, he stood and kicked the dent in the wall, causing flakes of paint to splinter and flutter to the floor. Bastian soon tired and noticed the crack running underneath the dent. But it didn't matter anymore; he'd soon be out of there. In a strange way, he felt just like the crack, as if his life had indeed fallen apart.

In his soul, he knew things. He knew that his love of coke was to blame. He knew he should quit, stay away altogether, but he couldn't get enough of it. He ran into the bedroom, rummaged in the drawers, and pulled out a tattered exercise book. Bastian licked a finger and scrolled through pages of graffiti-covered work for a number. He stopped when he found it. It was the name and number of an ex, Libby. They'd all partied at Blaq's until the night a grim trip converted her to Christianity.

A year ago, almost to the day, he had stood watch over her, not knowing how to make her feel better. She cried uncontrollably, frothed at the mouth, and made odd grunting noises. Then her skin prickled with heat, so she clawed at her body as if trying to remove clothes, not realising she was already naked. After that, a host of streaky red marks covered her body. At one point, she stopped, and her once frantic hands fell to her side. Then she curled into a ball and sobbed. Bastian made her as comfortable as he could and stayed with her, fearing that she wouldn't make it through the night. The next morning, she recovered in his arms and told him about her renewed belief in God. Maybe she'd remember his kindness rather than him dumping her for his new love.

Moments later, Bastian tore through the flat in search of change. He found a few coins down the back of the sofa and stumbled to the nearest phone box. Picking up the receiver, he inserted the money and dialled the number, his knuckles stark as he gripped the receiver, listening for the connection. He opened his mouth a few times, rehearsing what to say. However, the engaged tone that followed wasn't what he expected.

"Oh, shit... God," Bastian said, slamming the receiver into the cradle. He spun around in search of more money.

By chance, he stuck his finger in the phone and pulled out a fifty-pence piece, which he inserted and tried again. Libby picked up on the second ring. Bastian clutched the phone to his ear as if it were life support.

"Hey Bas, is it you? Are you OK? Where've you been?"

He cleared his throat, "I need help, Libby."

"You took off, and I didn't even know you weren't coming back, and now you call me out of the blue and—"

"I'm so sorry," he sniffed, pressed the phone to his ear, and wiped his leaking nose with his fingers.

"Don't know if I'll ever forgive you."

"Don't have anyone else, Lib. Been kicked out of the flat, and he's after me."

He combed his quiff with his fingers and leaned against the glass.

"Who?"

"White Boy Gator."

"What've you done now?"

Bastian told her what happened.

"He doesn't know where I live. Come," she said. "Don't worry; you'll be safe here."

"I'm never going to be able to pay him back, Lib. Don't have that kind of money."

Snorting, Bastian glanced up and down the road, checking for White Boy Gator. Afterwards, he wiped his nose with the bottom of his T-shirt

"Beg, borrow, or even steal to get here. We'll figure the rest out."

"Okay."

As the receiver slipped out of his sweaty hand, it clunked against the glass a few times, then dangled. Bastian's funk rose in waves from his armpits and stung his nostrils as he slumped to the bottom of the phone box. With his head in his hands, he sobbed. Then he pulled a ragged piece of once-white toilet paper from his jeans pocket and mopped at burning tears and snot. After a while, he came out of the phone box with puffy eyes and trudged home, his head down and hands jammed in his pockets.

As he turned into his road, he bumped into Blaq, who, upon hearing his plight, gave him money and invited him to score at a private party in Regent's Park.

As he freshened up, he looked in the mirror and patted the raised bump on his cheek. Staring at his reflection, he wondered if he should go straight to Libby's or have a farewell binge. Sticking a plaster over the bump, he decided on the party, convinced it was the last time and would cheer him up for the long trip to Epsom.

That night, Bastian and Blaq sauntered into the sumptuous townhouse full of glassy-eyed partygoers. Shadowy figures writhed naked in dark booths, enjoying the depths of their high, while others busied themselves minesweeping leftovers or eyeballing neat vodka. Bastian soon lost sight of Blaq, and for a moment, his heart skipped several beats when he thought he saw White Boy Gator. He darted behind a pillar and waited for his heart to resume normal pace. Bastian swore to himself when he saw it wasn't him. Hot, sweet relief filled him when he was approached by a scantily clad bar girl loaded with a leather belt full of complimentary tequila shots. Bastian drank like someone who had been deprived of water and charmed a statuesque blonde to find out where to score. She directed him further along the corridor where Bastian pushed open the door to the Velvet Lounge, and on a black marble table was a regular hell's buffet: an all-you-could-snort, pop or inject, pick 'n' mix of drugs.

Entranced by mound upon mound of white glory, it amazed Bastian that people snorted with rolled-up twenties and fifties or snorted fat lines straight from the table. He overheard some guys tripping about the Columbian, so he rubbed his hands and helped himself to a cut. Next, he headed to a loveseat in an alcove and tooted a short fat line. No one glanced in his direction as he spluttered and choked. The coke flew around the table like a miniature snowstorm. Then, right away, his nose dripped and red-rimmed eyes streamed, but he sorted himself out and tried again. Then, his nose was blocked, and he struggled to breathe. He blew his nose to get clear and tried again.

After two more lines, the thick, bitter nectar dribbled down the back of his throat. He licked a finger and dabbed the remaining powder on the table before rubbing it all over his gums. His heart sprinted as the coke surged through his body like water through the roots of a baobab tree before crashing into his brain. Then his eyes lit up, and the biggest grin spread across his face. Bastian feared no one, not even White Boy Gator.

*****

Libby remembered that night as if she was there, as when Bastian arrived, he couldn't stop going on about it. At first, it was the worst few weeks ever as he tried to get straight. His body became confused, and he felt sick. It all started with tremors and relentless headaches, followed by extreme hunger. After a while, things settled, and his condition improved. They read psalms that Bastian remembered and enjoyed worship songs and prayed. In no time, he looked like his old self.

One evening, Bastian popped out to buy milk. It was a trip that should have taken only ten minutes maximum, but half an hour passed, and he still had yet to return. Then, at last, Libby saw him. His light-footed swagger made him seem like he had no worries. As he neared the building, he dropped out of sight, but the key turned in the lock minutes later. Libby's voice came through the living room door.

"Finally."

Bastian stepped into the room and looked towards the window where Libby looked out into the darkness.

"Some old dear paying with coupons," he said.

She turned to study him and then smiled, "Bas, I worried."

"D-don't."

"Are you for real?" she asked, turning her back. "Bas, how're you really feeling?"

He sighed, "I'm all right."

Bastian moved a few strands of hair and kissed her neck. Libby turned, lifted her head, and kissed him on the lips. He smiled and hoped she couldn't see it was with his mouth, not his eyes. Bastian strolled into the kitchen, put the milk away, and returned to the living room.

"I really don't want to stress you out, Bas," she whispered. Her voice was steady, but he knew the tears weren't far behind.

"I guess I'm not over what you did. I thought you'd gone."

"Go?"

"Back to her, perhaps?"

"At least it wasn't a woman."

"It might as well have been. Wouldn't hurt so much as watching you destroy yourself and put your family through absolute hell."

"Yes, I did a little more than I should. Yes, I'm fucking stupid. Is that what you want me to say?" he asked her, surprised that he wanted to cry. "What could I do? We're not all strong like you, Libby." Then tears came, and he couldn't stop them.

"Sorry, Bas. But I'll never forget how..." she caught her breath, and Bastian realised she'd started crying, too.

"It tore my heart to shreds to see your Dad's face when you died for seven minutes. I mean, seven minutes."

"It's early days, but there's no going back," he paused. I mean, sometimes I even wonder what I was on. I wasn't brought up that way, but Tosh made me try it. Then we all did it together. It was just harmless fun."

Libby noticed the damp sweat patch under his arm as he ran his fingers through his quiff. Then he sighed and fell on the sofa as if he'd lost the use of his legs.

"But why didn't you just stop the *fun* when it started getting out of control?" she snapped, turning to face him.

"Drop it, Lib? It's over now," Bastian said. "*It's over*!"

"Bastian, Bas... I don't want you to end up six feet under. Can't you see that? Can't you get that into your head? Remember when they found that little boy's torso floating in the Thames?

That was no voodoo; that was White Boy Gator. Is that what you want?" She banged her mug on the table.

"Why so angry, Lib? I've never seen you like this before."

"Well, maybe it's time you did," she said, glaring at him. "Sometimes I wonder what's gotten into you. You've had everything handed to—"

"Thought the God vibes levelled you out, Lib?"

"You saw what happened to me — to us — and yet you do this." Bastian waited, not knowing if she'd finished. He looked at her in anguish.

"Lib, you don't think like that when it's got you." A lump rose in his throat. He picked up a box of Kleenex, took one, dabbed his eyes, and put the box on the floor. A piece of tissue clung to the corner of his eye.

"Why? I did it because I needed that. . . to be on top . . . in control." He tore off bits of wet tissue, rolled them into tiny balls, and dropped them on the floor.

"Any thoughts about the rent?"

Bastian moved to the sofa's edge, ran his fingers through his quiff, and snorted.

"With respect, screw the rent, Lib. It's White Boy Gator I've got to sort before he does me like the others."

"Well, my father's in France. I'll call him tomorrow."

"OK, thanks, Lib. I owe you big time."

The following night, Bastian vanished. His things were in place, but he wasn't. Someone had ripped out drawers and scattered the contents all over the place. The bed was a mess of crumpled sheets; they scattered clothes across the floor, but Bastian's toothbrush and toiletries were in their usual spots in the bathroom. It was as if he was in the middle of something and, like a Genie, up and disappeared. Neighbours reported Bastian struggling with a bunch of hench bouncers in the street. At first, they thought it was just horseplay until they witnessed someone matching White Boy Gator's description jostle him into a Jeep with blacked-out windows.

As days turned into weeks and months, sightings and searches led nowhere. After many phone calls, Libby told Bastian's parents what happened, and they informed the police. In the meantime, she visited some people and places he mentioned. She almost lost hope when Blaq called and told her Bastian was at one of White Boy Gator's dens working off his debt. She'd heard about the little missions — the kind that competed with demons in the closet and tormented the soul. When Libby spoke of plans to get him out, Blaq offered to round up foot soldiers and go with her. He despised White Boy Gator and was up for any opportunity to take him down.

They arrived at the block and took the pee-soaked lift to the seventh floor. Tension mounted as they approached the flat. They were in luck; there was no one on guard. The door was ajar. Blaq peeped in and saw nothing but darkness enhanced by taped black bin bags covering the windows. He pushed open the door and stepped inside. Libby huddled behind him, and Blaq's soldiers were a few paces back. Only shouts and gusts of sweet-burnt plastic rushed to greet them as they crept down the corridor. They sneaked past a room and listened to what sounded like White Boy Gator berating crack whores for holding out on him. In another room, on a 47-inch flat screen, a busty brunette's eyes opened wide, first with shock, then terror. She gagged as the well-oiled stud forced his huge penis down her throat. A clutch of oblivious crackheads squabbled over a pipe on its last legs.

A stocky, bald man emerged from a rear bedroom, adjusting his zipper and belt over a snug and bulging crotch as he strolled past them in the corridor. His gaze remained fixed on the threadbare carpet. There was only one room left, and Bastian had to be in there. Blaq and his foot soldiers stood guard outside the room in case White Boy Gator or his flying monkeys appeared. Libby inhaled deeply and pushed the door open without a sound. The first thing she noticed was a warm stench of stale semen mixed with sweet-smelling smoke.

"Bastian?"

It surprised her to hear how small her voice sounded. He did not reply and was transfixed by what he held in his hands.

Beads of perspiration glistened on Bastian's face. He shook, slumped forward, and a damp lock of hair flopped over glazed eyes. Libby tiptoed around him, mesmerised. A moth frittered around sturdy candles that blazed in a corner, creating flickering shadows on the wall. In the other corner sat a soiled mattress. To Bastian's left, on a makeshift nightstand, a furled fifty-pound note, used needles, cocaine-caked spoons, a bandanna, and a few crack wraps.

There was a time when he doubled for the guy from the Levi laundry ads. But that night, he stood a slip of his former self, peppered with bruises and scabs that resulted from coke bugs. Rising hot vapours singed the once salubrious eyelashes and eyebrows. Libby tried not to inhale the reek of singed hair. Bastian's once luscious lips were scorched from the hot, short pipe he pressed against them. Libby took her time, careful not to alarm him; her heart weighed down as if it might plummet like a boulder.

In the flickering light, it looked dark—brownish. But it was blood. A solitary trickle coursed down the back of a bony thigh as if escaping the site of the horror it had witnessed. It petered out before reaching the back of his knee. His boxers and jeans bagged around twig-like ankles. Bastian concentrated on the last of the crack trapped in the pipe screwed into his fist. It crackled and bubbled with a fusion of grey and white clouds. He raised the pipe to his lips, flicked the lighter, and inhaled the intoxicating aroma. His shoulders relaxed as the rush took effect.

"Bas," Libby said, "come, it's time to go."

He turned to her as if seeing her for the first time. His eyes filled with tears.

"I... can't."

Tell Him to Run

My heart races at a hundred miles per hour, with pain shooting through my chest. I grip the sides of the bed as the room spins. Dizziness overwhelms me, and my vision is blurred. I silently pray for Goodnews. Before I share what happened, please reserve judgment. I had no choice, but I'll tell you what happened while I still can.

It all began when they stormed in with machetes, reducing our homes to rubble. Once they had left, we sought refuge under the bridge along with hundreds of others. Dill often talked about finding a better place for us to live. Day after day, he shared his lofty dreams, convinced that we would soon have the life we had always longed for. The plan was for him to relocate first and then send for me and the children.

As time passed, people told me he fattened his eyes and fingers on the local women. One day, during Dill's visit, I gathered the courage to ask him, and I'm sure the children saw him sock me in the ribs. I doubled over, stifling a scream by cupping my mouth with my hand. Eventually, I realised it was wiser to play deaf, dumb and blind the next time I heard rumours. I even forced myself to believe that he did it because he was lonely without me. I clung to the hope that things would get better when we were all living together under one roof.

But after leaving the area under the bridge, our situation got even worse. It turned into a real-life nightmare. Back when our home by the river was still standing, we had plenty of fish—fish to eat, fish to smoke, and fish to sell. I often looked around the mud-baked hellhole with sludge-filled taps and wondered why. Why did I come here? What made it worse were the four-legged boarders with tails that crawled over us at night. One of them even bit Bim's baby toe.

Dill spent days on his bicycle, searching everywhere for water. Occasionally, he was lucky, but most of the time, he came back with empty cans. While some people prayed for money, my prayers involved clean water. At times, I felt like kicking myself. What kind of dream was this? What had he convinced me to believe in? We had little to look forward to but sex, and when we did, the babies followed. Since the hospital was far away, we would call Goodnews, who lived near the airport, if we needed further help.

A few months after Bim was born, Dill pulled away from me. I suppose it was sheer frustration. Every time he turned around, he only saw gaping black holes and never had enough of anything to feed them. He grew weary of hearing, "Baba, I'm hungry." Also, he hated the fact that I often mocked his dream.

"You know something? Without me, you're nothing," his bony face tight like a fist in a leather glove. "You are what they call a parasite." His hands cast bird-like shadows on the wall as he shook them vigorously.

Then, he turned away and put on his one dashiki. My eyes drilled into him. What did he mean? How could he say that? My legs gave way, and I slumped back in the chair. Then, there was silence. I wasn't sure, but I heard a sound in his throat as he wiped his eyes. Dill never cried. I could barely talk; it was as if I'd swallowed blades. All that came out was, "Shut up." My voice was shaky. "You sent for us. You promised us a better life!" Dill clenched his fists, punched a wall, and stormed out to meet with his brothers.

He was the parasite, the one who did really evil things to make ends meet with his demonic brothers, Boi and Gator. They would enter people's homes in broad daylight without masks and rob them with guns and knives, whether or not the occupants were present. Once, they hijacked a bus and taxed the people with money and jewellery. For those without money, they went to the extent of chopping their arms and legs. While Dill recounted, he threw his head back and roared with laughter, taunting me about the gushing blood, exposed flesh, and white bone.

The graphic details he described, coupled with the sound of his laughter, really turned my stomach. It seemed inevitable that the Boys would catch up with them, and they would soon face the consequences they deserved.

When I confided in Pastor, he said, "Ashes fly in the face of him who throws them."

Money never found us, so I took the children to the dump to sift through rubbish, glass, toxic waste, and plastic bottle tops until they dragged their feet. I sold whatever I could, which kept us going, but I knew my children needed more. Their ribs all jutted out, and hunger filled their eyes like night in the bush, especially Bim, who often vomited bile. My baby needed water and often woke in pain at night. His tummy always poked out. Every morning, I thanked God for blessing him with another day. As months passed, I grew tired of the constant smell of diesel and rubbish everywhere. Sanitation was so poor that people shit in the open — even in the water. Thoughts of escape played on a loop in my mind day and night.

I needed to find a way out—perhaps the answer lay overseas. Time was running out for me, but at least the children could have a shot at a better life.

One night, as I slept, Dill pulled at the sheet. I clung on with all my strength and asked him to stop. I dozed off, only to wake up to the same unwelcome behaviour. There were no tender kisses of lips, neck or whispers — just him saying, "Come on, now," and placing his leg across my body. With fiery breath, he got on top, attempting to have his way, but I fought. We struggled for a while, and I begged him to leave me alone. Eventually, he ended up at the edge of the bed. In his attempt to return, he reached over to grab me, but I rolled away. After a while, he chain-smoked cigarettes at the foot of the bed, putting out the butts on the floor with his bare heel. He had witnessed what happened to those who encountered the Boys, and he was clearly worried about being hunted by them. They had caught wind of Dill's evil escapades and were planning with a mob to track him, Boi, and Gator down in the street and teach them a lesson they would never forget in this life or the next. In short, he needed a way out.

"Yana, you must take a trip!"

"What about my children?" I said, tucking the surrounding sheet.

"Do not question me!"

See, his plan was for me to have an operation. As he explained the details, a lump lodged in my throat, and the sweat-drenched sheet clung to my back. Each time I refused, he'd choke me. It had become such a routine that he knew precisely when to release his grip. While I lay there coughing — choking and trying to catch my breath, he threatened to sell my children if I didn't cooperate. What could I do? There was no choice but to go along with his plan. After things had settled down, my heart leapt into my mouth when I heard my children shouting with their tiny fists thumping on the other side of the wall.

Dill said he'd go with me as if he doubted trusting me. So, at first light, he called Goodnews to inform him that we were on our way. Sitting in the back of the car, I couldn't stop wondering if I was making the right decision. I prayed for God's strength repeatedly; my mind couldn't focus on anything else.

When we arrived, Goodnews directed me to a tiny, damp room. In one corner, an oversized generator took up space. On the opposite wall, broken blinds clinked in the window, and beneath it, there was a tall bed resembling some kind of meat block. Broken taps lay under the sink, and Goodnews had scattered jars, pipes, and bric-à-brac all over the floor. Seconds later, he tossed a sheet at me and instructed me to take off my clothes. First, he attempted to wash his hands with the unclean water from the tap before struggling into a small pair of ink-stained rubber gloves. Then, he hurried me onto the bed, boasting that the operation was a first, something that had never been attempted anywhere in the world.

Thoughts of the operation really terrified me. Fear churned in my stomach, and I wanted desperately to use the toilet, but I hadn't even eaten. Before I knew it, Goodnews' unsteady hands grappled with a needle. I held my breath as it stabbed, pierced, and tugged at my skin before penetrating the back of my hand. Goodnews counted back from ten and reached five. I blacked out.

When I came to, I was relieved to be alive but also felt a deep loneliness. I scanned the room and then reflected on what had happened. The reality hit when Goodnews leaned over the bed, chewing gum.

"You did well, Yana. A success."

I wasn't so sure, mainly because of the pain. As a child, my parents taught me never to wish ill upon others, but at that moment, I hated Dill with a vengeance. When I opened my mouth to speak, Goodnews shoved a tablet between my lips, and before I knew it, I passed out. When I woke up, I wondered why I couldn't see my toes. As I looked up, a spider dropped from the ceiling like a secret assassin. Lifting my arm to swipe it away, an incredible pain shot through me, questioning my sanity. I blew air, and the spider disappeared. When I turned to look for it, I couldn't believe the tightness across my chest. I decided not to move. Seconds later, I forgot when something tickled my nose and I tried to scratch it. Not even halfway there, once again, the pain stopped any movement. I kept my arms by my side, closed my eyes, and fell asleep.

After a while, my constant groaning made Goodnews give me another couple of tablets to ease the pain before he left the room. The generator broke the silence and roared to life with its black noise. Two minutes later, I stared up at the ceiling, counting holes in the off-white tiles. Then, I noticed something. At first, it seemed like another hole, but it moved. I was sure it moved. It was a baby spider that reminded me of my Bim. Sweet little Bim with eyes like the moon and his little wrinkled elbows. Forget Dill. I had to go through with the plan for my children—for Bim's sake. Anyway, I had no choice as the operation was over, and the thing was already inside of me. Watching the little spider and thinking of Bim helped me to focus on something other than the ache in my breasts.

Why so much pain? I wanted to bawl for Mama, just like Bim bawls for me when he's hungry. After hearing my moans, Goodnews reappeared in the doorway with a handful of tablets. He assured me not to worry, that the pain would soon go, and I could travel.

After quickly taking the tablets, it took a few minutes for them to work. Soon after, I could almost think straight. I agonised over the task ahead but prayed for God's guidance. While I gathered my thoughts, Dill, Boi, and Gator sat and raved about the operation being a blessing, claiming that the government had tightened security at the airport. They insisted I leave after a few days, even though I didn't feel up to it. Dill, Boi, and Gator helped me slide off the bed and into the car. Goodnews waved me away with a bottle of tablets I would take every few hours. When we got home, I went to bed and stayed there while the girls attended to my every need.

When the big day came, it seemed like an ordinary day with a blue sky and hot weather, but nothing was ordinary. The night before, I told the children about my plane trip to buy them nice things. They were so excited. Then, I took some tablets so I could put them to bed without too much pain. I spent a long time tucking them in and watching them fall asleep. After a while, I left them and packed. I couldn't stop the tears from coming. Around midnight, I returned to the children and tickled their nostrils to wake them up. I just needed to hold them one more time. Just one more time. They were sleepy, bodies like rag dolls, but I made them stay awake and play with me. When they tired, I kept kissing them until they wiped their faces and pushed me away. Some time after, Dill appeared in the doorway, yanked them away from me, and whisked them to his mother's house.

Before long, Boi and Gator hammered on the door. Boi stormed in and buzzed around like a tsetse fly, checking out all areas and pulling the curtains. He told me to take off my clothes so he could examine my breasts. Reluctantly, I stripped, hoping Dill would say something, but he didn't. Boi moved closer to touch my breasts. I stumbled backwards, and the pain of a thousand sharp needles shot through me. My breasts throbbed, red and hot. Days before, flattened eggplants lolled on my tummy, but I looked down, and my eyes told no lies. I tilted as the hefty things pulled on my back, neck and shoulders. Without offering me, Dill filled three glasses to the brim with wine. The brothers clinked glasses, swallowed in a gulp, and hugged each other like small children at a party.

I'll never forget how Boi bounced around the room as if he had come into untold riches.

"It's not possible... It's not possible," he said, rubbing his hands together.

They guzzled more wine and plotted what-ifs while I shuffled around serving them food. I so wanted to sink my teeth, but couldn't eat a thing. They talked of how they planned to spend thousands of dollars in between mouthfuls.

Later, Boi and Gator took us to the airport and waited outside. Redness under closed lids confirmed the murderous heat as the sun danced on top of my head. Boi handed us passports, tickets, money and spat rapid-fire instructions we were to follow to the letter. Just to be sure, I swallowed a few tablets to keep myself pain-free for at least a few hours. He told us to stick together and warned that he would follow closely behind. However, when we entered, Dill instructed me to meet him at the departure gate. Inside, people were frantically grabbing at each other's throats over muddled bags caused by a power failure. Sweat poured down in streams as I lugged my bag past them.

I stared as people waited for scanning. Hurrying to the toilet, I locked myself in a cubicle and sat on the lid, panting. Panic set in, and my heart pounded. I held my breath then exhaled before doing breathing exercises to calm down, expecting the guards to burst in and drag me out. No one came in, so I yanked some tissue and dabbed at the sweat. I popped out of the cubicle, and it was only when I looked in the mirror that I realised bits of tissue had stuck to my face. I raced back into the cubicle as people came in. When they finished and left, I used the toilet, flushed, and went to the sink. Looking into the mirror, I couldn't believe the state I was in. I ran the tap and drenched my face in cold water. Someone pushed the door open, so I rushed back into the cubicle.

When I calmed down, I peeped under the door to check the toilet was empty, then stepped out with an icy chill trickling down my spine. After a few minutes, the scanning stopped. I bent under the dividers and made my way along the corridor.

Upon reaching the departure lounge, I showed my passport and boarding card. I heard shouting. An officer ran with flailing arms in my direction, but as he got closer, my pounding heart was all I could hear. My bag slipped out of my fingers and hit the floor. I waited. Nothing happened. The officer brushed past me, causing me to stumble. He grabbed a young man's arm, commanding him to remove his shoes. They were a pair of thick rubber-soled leathers. The officer ordered him to put them on the conveyor belt, and the man refused. 'Since some fool tried to carry explosives in the sole of his shoes, now we all have to take ours off,' I thought. Feeling faint from the heat, hunger, and fear, I grabbed the desk for support. A steward crouched beside me.

"Do you need help?"

"No, no, no, I'm fine," I said, forcing myself upright. I showed my passport and then heard a voice ask if she had searched me. I turned to face someone I knew would be thorough. She ushered me back to the scanning area, where I emptied my pockets down to the white balls of fluff in the lining.

The tray moved along the conveyor and through the X-ray, where a sweaty, fat man drenched in sweat hogged the screen. When it was my turn to pass through, I took off everything I thought might trigger the alarm. I didn't want to give them any reason to investigate. I joked as they started the routine: feet shoulder-width apart, arms out, and palms up. The woman patted down the front and back of my dress. I winced as her clumsy hands moved over my breasts. Then, I had to lift my arms again. As I did, my bitterness tingled in my nostrils, and I hoped it put her off, but no such luck. Someone shouted, so she stopped and answered. I dropped my arms. She told a man to continue the search. Looking around, I saw Boi signal to the man, who then told me I could go. Taken aback, I felt as though my ears were playing tricks on me. I stared at him as if I hadn't heard. He repeated himself. Breathing a sigh of relief, my heart fluttered. God's grace was good.

Then the dog came.

I gulped.

It sniffed everybody: bags, shoes, babies. Everything.

"Please, God, no, please, no," I thought. I knew if I moved away, it would look odd, so I prayed under my breath. The dog trotted over to me and sniffed my dress and feet before trotting off. God forbid bad things. I sighed. It scampered over to a man and buried its nose in the side of his rucksack. An officer marched over to investigate. He held up something, and I heard mention of overseas threats and disease. The officer patted the dog's head, then the dog pulled away from him and meandered back to me through a mass of people. It plopped down at my feet.

The officer followed.

"You have narcotics?"

"Me? No, no," I said.

"Please come with me." He grabbed my arm, but I snatched it back. Another officer took my passport and ticket, scrutinising them. Afterwards, he handed them to another officer in plain clothes. I scanned for Boi. The officer called yet another officer.

My bag bounced against my leg as they led me to an interview room.

"You want to talk?" said the first hawkish officer.

"No," I said.

"Trying to hide something?" he said, "Tell me that!" He stepped forward, making it clear he was the boss.

"No."

"Don't waste my time," he said.

"I'm not."

"Something's up."

I turned away, my eyes desperately searching through the crowds for Boi.

"You spiking," the officer cackled. "We'll find out when we search."

"I've got nothing," I said.

Then, I wished for the ground to open up and swallow me on the spot.

"I'm going to see my family," I said, looking around. A woman approached and read my rights, asking if I understood. They called the police, who escorted me to a room where they ordered me to undress. A few minutes later, I stood naked but for the stream of sweat that ran between my breasts. Rough hands examined me, and I would've turned every shade of red, if possible. I knew the end neared when they said I had to go to the hospital for an internal examination.

After getting dressed, I needed to go to the toilet. The guards walked too close on either side of me, their necks erect like striking cobras. I remembered what Boi said should anything go wrong, and as I came out of the toilet, a commotion kicked off. The guards shot from my side to see what was going on. At first, I thought the ruckus was because someone refused a search, but my jaw dropped when I saw Dill.

Dill wiped his forehead, then sprang and thrust his finger in their faces. Bullets of sweat dripped, and his eyes were wide open. An officer pushed him with one hand and warned with the baton in the other. Dill's tall, but they loomed, braced to lash his head. I carried on walking, but for a split second, I turned back, and our eyes locked. In a matter of seconds, he cuffed one in the face before more guards moved in to deal with him. Although wiry, Dill could punch through sand. I prayed he did. I really did.

I scanned for Boi while Dill kept them busy. Heading to the exit, the coppery taste of fear filled my mouth. As I approached the doors, they *opened and closed, opened and closed, opened and closed*. My head throbbed as someone called out. I wanted to sprint, but sharp shooting pains and muscle spasms in my chest stopped me. Pushing on, I hurried past guards who didn't know what was happening and the blur of a million faces watching. Red blobs floated in front of my eyes. I almost felt like time was slipping away, the seconds dripping like water through my fingers. The heartbeat in my chest echoed louder, matching the buzz in the air. I quickened my pace, navigating through the crowd, the sea of faces and outfits merging into a colourful blur.

All at once, a guard approached. To my right, Boi and Gator. Something glistened in Gator's hand. He pointed at the guard. As I walked by, an officer grabbed him from behind, wrestling him to the ground. I dashed to the doors as three bangs rattled my bones. Just before I passed through, everything blacked. I put my hands out in front. The power outed, and the sliding doors froze open. I don't remember how, but Boi got ahead of me. Before I knew it, he had stuffed me into the car and sped away. That's all I remember.

The generator shot to life, waking me up. It hummed like an amplified mosquito. A few moments later, the noise died. And I remembered the where, how, and why. The tablets made me groggy, and my lips were dry and cracked. One by one, I got bits of skin — between my lips and teeth — and pulled, ripping them off. Then, I used the little air I had left to spit them out. Where was Dill? Boi said he'd come.

The sun was a gigantic ball of fire that lit everything as it set. Silhouettes of people were milling in the road. I hoped for Dill, prayed he'd come and take me home to my children. Out of nowhere came shouts that sounded close to the window. Boi peeped through the blinds, then shot outside, slamming the door. I watched the door, then struggled to peek through the blinds, praying no one saw me. Boi took off like a rocket as if he was trying to catch up with someone. Behind him, the Boys' mob sprinted, too, as if they were on a mission. Soon, I couldn't distinguish Boi from the others.

"Stop!" they shouted.

They blasted Boi with sticks and rocks as he zigzagged in the road. When he tripped and fell, some mob members crowded around and finished him. The other wiry man continued to sprint for his life. Something struck me about his top. It was a colourful dashiki. It reminded me of Dill. After a few moments, the penny dropped. I saw it was Dill. My heart pounded as he buckled — betrayed by wiry legs — fell and rolled head over heels into a ball. I knew his fate. He knew, too, because he tucked his head and hugged his knees close to his chest. The mob leaned in and pounded him without mercy.

After a while, the leader of the Boys shouted and raised his hand to stop the baying crowd's assault. He bent over, rolled Dill onto his bottom, drew his fist back, and then slugged him to the ground.

"You had a choice," said the leader standing over him.

Dill tried to get up on his elbow, but his arm hung like a sock filled with rice.

"S-sorry," he said, wiping at strings of blood and spit with the knuckles of the good hand.

"Him." someone grunted. "It's him. One of the men chopping on the bus!"

The leader cursed, spat in the dirt, and then left Dill. He jogged to a tree and hacked the bark with a machete. A man on a motorbike flicked on a radio, and a track about water blared. The leader yanked at fresh pieces of bark while crowd members sang along and clapped to the water track. Meanwhile, a meagre one forced Dill to sit up. He called some others. I didn't want to look as I felt like I was going to vomit.

Dill stretched his good arm to the sky.

"God, don't let them kill me. Yana, my children." he cried.

I could no longer think straight. I'd finished the tablets, and the dress felt like it was getting tighter by the minute. When my neck stiffened, I turned to face the wall but could still hear them. When I turned to look again, they had slashed Dill and his clothing to shreds. Blood splashed everywhere in the road. The mob chanted while threading him through two tyres. My heart tripped.

"*Tell him to run*," I uttered to no one but God.

Minutes later, angry villagers gathered. Some lusted for blood with their nut heads full of pot and wine. Others stood by the side in protest — teeth like the whitest yam. A man yawned on the corner. A group of small children stood and pointed while a few elders, deep in conversation, hung their heads and sloped off. The sky changed to a reddish tint with strips of dark clouds, but I could still see what and who.

A boy with an afro grabbed a can of petrol and held it away from his body before splashing Dill from the top of his head to his foot bottom. The leader set fire to bits of bark and hurled them at Dill. Flashes of red, orange and dark grey spun through the air and landed on the tyre's lip. Dill shrieked before exploding into a fireball. Arrows of smoke shot into the sky. The smell of burning rubber tinged with flesh hung in the already thick air. If I hadn't seen it with my own eyes, the scent would have led me to think rubber burned on a barbeque. I stared at them, shaking — monsters! How could they murder another human being?

Fire flickered in their faces, and they looked like masks for a moment. Dill thrashed for a while before the fight had gone. I prayed for his strength, but his stick-thin arms stuck fast to his sides. I retched as if bringing up my guts, but there was nothing. Nothing. I wished I could help him, but I couldn't. I had to calm myself down and concentrate to breathe. As I looked on, my heart flipped, and not long after, I heard screaming, but I took a moment to realise it came from deep down inside of me. I cried for Dill until I could only croak. The stubs of my nails clung to the sides of the bed.

After a while, Dill merged with the tyres, frozen by flames in a charred black heap. My throat burned as boiling tears rolled down my face and cooled in my ears. For a minute, my nose blocked, but when I sniffed, my nostrils cleared, and I smelled him. The bitter odour seeped through cracks in the window, door and floor. I struggled to lift my head as if to stop from drowning, but the odour covered me like a blanket. It was as if he had come back for me after all.

Through half-closed eyes, I studied the door. Like night falling, a wave of drowsiness begged to take me beyond sleep. My body relaxed, eyelids heavy, hands and legs numb. I struggled to open my eyes and knew that darkness would soon come for good. As Goodnews crashed through the door, I noticed a sharp, citrus smell. It stood out above the mustiness in the room. Oranges. It was definitely oranges. And I remembered the day. I remembered the orange. I had never seen anything like it.

It was the yellowest orange I had ever seen. One afternoon, Dill set off on his bike to find water. Days later, he returned holding a mouldy orange like a diamond in the palm of his hand. The rotten scent filled the air. Dill gave it to me, but Bim tried to take it from my hand. I wasn't sure if he should eat it, but it was all we had. Bim pulled at my fingers as I opened it for him. Red juice oozed over my hands, the smell growing stronger than ever. The dark insides resembled raw meat with blood. Bim couldn't wait, his eyelids quivering.

"Mama, gi' mi," he said, reaching for the orange. I pulled him close, slid my arms under his, and lifted him onto my lap. His eager body trembled against mine. He seized the orange with both hands, tore into the rot, and smiled from ear to ear.

Behaving Badly

Mrs. Gator summoned me to her office, letting me know that my parents would take me out for the day instead of going home for the weekend. I was a little surprised, to say the least

It was July 21st. I sat on the stone steps, leaning on the big butterfly doors, enjoying the fresh air. Going to boarding school sucked; it felt like torture. I would've rather gone to prison. No matter how much I told my parents I hated it, they didn't want to discuss it. I cried into my pillow most nights, even after they said I'd get used to it. I tried giving it time, but things got worse, and memories of Summer kept coming back. Boarding school felt like punishment for what happened to her. After that mess, my parents believed sending me away was the solution, but it did nothing for the chaos in my head. Instead, my thoughts went from bad to worse. If only they could understand that I only had their best interests at heart.

The staff had a sit-down with my parents, bringing up social anxiety and depression and suggesting a psychologist. I went along, playing the part, but I never really let her in. Trusting her was a hurdle; there was something about her that kept me guarded. It was hard to believe she didn't think I was bad in some way. Soon enough, they handed me a prescription for anti-depressants. At first, I took them out of curiosity, wishing they'd cast a numbness over my situation. Initially, they appeared to work, shoving the dark thoughts aside and giving me a rose-tinted view of life.

I felt lighter, less troubled, and could interact with people. However, I soon noticed that while they helped with one thing, they made me feel too exhausted to do much of anything and gave me horrid headaches, among other more personal issues. So, I just stopped taking them. Apparently, it's the worst thing you could do. The darkness returned with full force, and I turned into an absolute terror among the others whom I labelled as 'inmates.'

Once again, I griped to my parents that things would completely unravel unless they took me out and let me come home. Unfortunately, they turned a deaf ear and wouldn't stop nagging me about taking those chunky tablets. I took them all right and kept them together in my pocket. I grabbed a handful, felt their chalkiness in my sweaty palm, and then tucked them away again.

With my eyes closed, I inhaled deeply, relishing the sun's warmth on my face. When I opened my eyes, a Peregrine falcon perched on a distant building caught my attention. Research from the library painted them as powerful creatures with distinctive, eagle-like wings. As I admired the falcon, my gaze shifted to my Wolverine boots, and an unexpected sense of strength surged within me.

They were perfect for trudging along Brighton Beach. I mean, it wasn't your typical beach with flip-flops or hot sand between your toes. Without a doubt, doing that might land you in the hospital. Brighton was famous for its pebble beach that made such a racket and caused your feet to sink with every step. While it was excellent exercise for the heart and calf muscles, it wasn't too good for old fogies like my parents. I made a mental note to keep an eye on them.

A few minutes later, my parents arrived. I was pleased to see them, but Mum, not so much, as she was the one who insisted that I should stay at the boarding school. On the other hand, Dad seemed more supportive, perhaps due to his private meetings with a young female client. I had walked into his office and stumbled upon them in what adults called a compromising position. I chose not to tell Mum because I might be able to get him to persuade her to let me return home. I hopped into the backseat and stuck my head between them.

"Where are we going then?" I said, trying to read their body language.

"Did you take your tablets, Wynter?"

"Of course, Mum."

"There's a good boy."

I squeezed the tablets nesting in the lint in my pocket. Soon, we were on our way, winding through charming villages and beautiful trails crowded with tourists and bizarrely dressed people. I often wished we lived in Brighton, but my parents said they couldn't afford it. Just imagine living in one of those Regency houses with grand columns and balconies. It must be nice to gaze at the sea from your bedroom window or watch the seagulls as they dipped and dived, soaring high above the waves.

Anyway, reflecting on it now, I wish we had never stopped for the hiker. Yes, I kicked the back of Dad's chair, but only because I didn't want him to stop. Yes, I know it was a bad idea. And yes, I know it confirmed Dad and Mum's thoughts about me, but it would've saved us a lot of time and trouble if only he'd listened to me.

So, there we were out in good old Brighton AND Hove, apparently. It was a common belief that you'd get your tongue pulled out if you only said "Brighton." My parents chose it because it wasn't too far to get me back to the boarding school, and to be honest, I'd researched it and found out that it was called the 'queen of slaughtering places' in the thirties. I quite liked that.

Some loonies murdered, chopped up and stored people in trunks and suitcases. I must admit, I found that fascinating for all the right reasons. Also, I liked Brighton Pier because it had a funfair, slot machines, candy floss, fish and chips, and Brighton Rock. The last time, I secretly stashed a stick of rock in my pocket. Later, when I was alone, I sucked that thing until it became a lethal weapon.

Anyway, soon, it was lunchtime, and we were ready for fish and chips. I had a thing about chip shop chips and fish so fresh like it had just been pulled out of the sea.

I prayed it wasn't from the Brighton one, though, because that was definitely polluted. But to be honest, it hadn't killed me yet, so what the hell. They said what didn't kill fattened. I could work with that. Anyway, afterwards, I had a healthy dollop of chocolate cake with chocolate custard. Then, we shuffled along the Pier, lugging plastic bags full of copper and brass to nourish the machines. We knew they were rigged, but we still had fun playing.

It was well after six when we had emptied our bags and headed to the car. Dad was in a hurry to return; he said he was expecting a call from someone. I wondered if Mum knew about the someone. Sliding into the backseat, I felt tired from all the excitement. I marvelled at the waning sunset, a picture-perfect blend of charcoal and orange stripes.

The sky darkened in a matter of minutes, and rain chucked it down, really thrashing Dad's windscreen wipers until they were on their knees. Noisy dark sheets of the stuff sloshed from the heavens, and for a minute, it was like being stuck in a high-powered jet wash. A beautiful double rainbow filled the sky when it passed, and we could see the road ahead. In Eastern culture, a double rainbow was a sign of good fortune. The first one was about achieving riches, and the second was more geared towards the spiritual side of things. So, good news all around. How exciting!

But out of nowhere, a figure appeared at the side of the road with hands clenched at the sides. As we approached, a pale thumb showed they needed a lift, and then we saw the downcast eyes that pleaded with us to stop. It was a young girl. I wondered where she came from; there was nothing and no one for miles. Why was she out there on her own? What did she really want?

"We can't," Dad said. "I'll be late."

Mum replied, "Why not? She's on her own. You wouldn't want Sum... me to be out there like that, would you?"

Dad said nothing, but I looked in the mirror, and there was an answer in his eyes that needed no words. He's such a strange one sometimes, the way he looks at me–at Mum.

And the other thing about him was that he knew how to scrutinise galore! I think I've inherited it, too. But to be honest, that's mainly because of my twin, Summer's unfortunate death a few years ago.

The coroner concluded it was by misadventure, and thank God for that. Even though Summer was a royal pain in the arse most of the time, we all missed her terribly. Summer used to be all sparkly eyes, peaches and cream with rosy cheeks before the fang and claw episode. Something made her go a bit "Gothy," and she developed a fascination with mythical creatures, then forked out for permanent vampire fangs. Before bedtime, she'd creep into my room, make hissing noises, and tell me she could smell my blood from a distance and how she would love the taste. Underneath the dinner table, she used to prod me with that chrome-tip nail thing she had, always trying to draw my blood. But she couldn't really get at me because I was always swift... swift, like a falcon. But I worried about Dad and Mum. Sometimes, Summer would go to extremes to get their attention, too. She was the epitome of a philistine, cursing them like a real trooper and scribbling things about murdering them in the vilest ways possible. I mean, they didn't know, but I took it upon myself to watch her because something told me she was hell-bent on doing something to them. Something had to give.

The night Summer came to an end, waves of nausea rushed through me, but I was sure I did the right thing. Her passing was a massive loss that Dad and Mum battled daily. They had so much hope for us, the twins. See, they had the rose-tinted idea that we would always have each other. On the one hand, it was a blessing, but in my and Summer's case, it was definitely a curse. They spent the following year convinced I'd lost my marbles; their eyes always questioned, but I told them I blacked out and couldn't remember what happened.

Anyway, Mum put her foot down about giving the hiker a lift, and Dad had to take heed, morphing into wilted lettuce. He didn't slow down quickly enough, so Mum rained punches on his arm to encourage him a little. He sunk the brake to the floor, and there was a loud clicking sound as he pulled up the handbrake.

Then I leaned forward to get a better look at the hiker. I kicked Dad's chair and whispered through my teeth, "Please, keep going." I don't know why, but I just had a bad feeling about her. But he didn't listen.

Rain lashed down again, accompanied by thunder and occasional flashes of lightning. The hiker bent her head against the wind and rain, clutching her coat, and jogged to the car. Mum pressed the button, and the window went down.

"Where are you going?"

"There," she pointed.

"Where's there?"

"Portslade."

Now, what she said was only a few miles away. Mum said little else, and Dad's ears were a livid red.

"Satisfied?" he mumbled under his breath.

"What?" she said.

"How was she planning on getting there?" he asked.

"Oh, give it a rest, will you, Robert!"

"But... should we... Uhm... with Wynter... in the back?"

"He's fine."

"Look, if anything goes left, it's on you!"

"But he's taken his tabs... we're going in that direction, aren't we, love?"

"Marie."

Dad spoke Mum's name quietly under his breath, but it was too late.

"Thanks," the hiker said. She opened the back door and got in beside me. I scooted up towards the window and stared at her. When she looked in my direction, I turned my head quickly and peered out of the window.

I caught a glimpse of Dad's eyes in the mirror, and he looked worried. Perhaps it was because the road was deserted, with no other cars in sight, no street lamps, or anything. And then comes a hiker, just like in the movies. I felt afraid. Afraid of what she might do. I could hear her breathing. It sounded like her nose was blocked up. She lifted her nostrils and sniffed, then kept sniffing.

It made me feel uneasy. Hikers are always baddies in the movies, aren't they?

The smell of wet earth was strong in the back of the car. As Dad pulled out, I couldn't help but watch as the hiker shook her hair loose. I stole another glimpse, trying to make out her face. I gulped. Something inside me shrank. To me, she looked like an ultra-white version of Summer. I had a flashback and remembered what Summer looked like lying in her coffin. Like Summer, the hiker looked like she hadn't seen the sun for a long while. Her shaky alabaster hands rested on her knees.

"Had a nice day?" she asked.

I shook my head back and forth. "I..."

"Yes." For some reason, Mum was loud, as if to drown out Dad, who hadn't said a word. I closed my eyes.

"We've been down by the Pier... had a lovely fish and chip brunch, and the price wasn't half bad."

"Oh, yeah." The hiker looked over at me. I could've sworn she mouthed something else. But I couldn't be sure.

Dad cleared his throat, "So, where are you from?"

"Erm... my boyfriend... we had a row... back there."

Something seemed strange. I was about to open my mouth at that exact moment, but I thought I saw something flash in her eyes.

"What's your name, love?" Mum asked.

"Jeanie."

She smiled. "He yours?"

"Yep, that's our boy..."

I said nothing.

"You all right?" The hiker turned to me, so I twisted my body to the window. Suddenly, my eyes widened, and my heartbeat quickened. I jumped when I felt something sharp on my leg, like maybe the chrome tip of a nail. She giggled. It was Summer's giggle. Definitely Summer's giggle. Panic surged within me. Shifting in my seat, my breaths came quicker as beads of sweat formed on my forehead. A shiver ran down my spine, and my breath caught in my throat. What on earth was I going to do?

"Don't!" That was all I could muster.

"Glad we left when we did!" Dad interrupted.

"Hmm," Mum said.

As we passed a street lamp, I peeped at the hiker, who had her head in her hands. What was going on? The panic rose again. I felt my legs go weak, and my palms were clammy.

I clung to the back of Dad's chair.

"Dad, I need to pee."

The car ploughed on through the rain.

"Dad, I need... you need to stop somewhere, I need to go."

He just looked in the rear-view mirror at me and mumbled something to Mum about me having a panic attack.

Soon enough, we pulled into a petrol station, and we all got out. The hiker ran to the toilet. I clung to Mum and told her my fears. She said I should stop being silly, or I'd never come home. I'd do anything not to return to the boarding school.

We returned to the car with water, hot chocolate, and petrol station hotdogs. As I sat in the corner, my legs shook. I wiped the sweat on my palms on my jeans and checked the time. I needed to do something to make them take me home. I took a deep breath. I only had a few hours to execute my plan. But what was the plan?

When I couldn't spot the hiker anywhere, a wave of relief washed over me. I released a long sigh, and my shoulders dropped. Dad and Mum adjusted their seatbelts. As I settled in, Dad switched on the engine. To my surprise, the hiker was tucked in the corner like she had never been out. I yelped, spilling my hot chocolate in my lap. My mouth felt dry, and the hotdog had rolled under Dad's chair.

I'm sure the hiker grinned at me. Did I see vampire fangs? My heart leapt into my throat. Looking into the mirror, I tried to alert Dad and Mum, but they were at each other's throats about whether or not I had *really* taken my tablets. I kicked at the back of Dad's chair, trying to get his attention. However, he ignored me and continued to assert his manhood with Mum. I didn't know what else to do.

I kept my eyes on the hiker as I pressed myself back into the corner and wiped the sweat on my neck and forehead. I couldn't breathe; my stomach felt twisted in knots. I drew my feet up and hugged my knees to my chest, with my heels on the seat. The hiker moved her hand, and I thought she was reaching out for me again, so I shrank back so small she couldn't touch me. I closed my eyes tight as memories of Summer rushed back. I shook as a wave of panic settled over me like a shroud. I had no choice but to do something. But what? I wished I had more preparation time before she got into the car. I had to act fast to save my parents.

As I reflected on my research about the 'loonies,' an unsettling urge surged within me. I felt the desire to tackle her, to squash any potential threat. The thought of her face meeting the road flickered in my mind, reminding me of Mash Gets Smash, an old advert featuring Martians and Daleks Mum once showed me on YouTube. A grin crept across my face as I glanced in Dad's mirror.

"What's so funny?" he asked.

"Nothing."

"You're grinning like a Cheshire."

"Am I?"

"Come on, share the joke, son."

"Nothing." I stopped grinning. Dad gave me a stern look, and I knew what it meant.

"It had better be!"

Waves of nausea rippled once again, and my head throbbed. I spied that the hiker's door latch was in the open position. My Wolverine boots were ready. I figured if I was swift... swift like a falcon, I could yank the handle...

... and kick her out.

That's what the voice in my head told me to do. I giggled, trying to stop my shoulders from going up and down, but it was hard to do. I couldn't help sniggering, causing a snot bubble to shoot out of my nose.

"What's going on back there?" Dad said.

Glancing at the hiker, then at the door latch, I reached over and released it. The door flew open. Totally shocked, the hiker screamed. She hung on as I raised a Wolverine boot to help her out. As Dad's tyres screeched to a halt, a tense silence hung in the air. The hiker, still clinging on, locked eyes with me, her expression a mix of fear and determination. As Dad opened his door, the hiker let go and stumbled away from the car.

Dad, his face a mix of confusion and concern, hurriedly stepped out, trying to understand the chaotic scene. Meanwhile, Mum, wide-eyed, demanded an explanation. I took a deep breath, quickly spinning a tale about the hiker trying to strangle them. The hiker, now standing at a distance, eyed us warily before staggering off. Nervous and confused, I unscrewed the lid on the water bottle, scooped out a couple of tablets, and swallowed. Tipping my head back, I prayed they bought my version of events. I closed my eyes. I really wanted to go home.

BLACKBALLED
8
M. HENNINGHAM

Coming soon... BLACKBALLED.

This Deliciously Dark Short Story collection features five tales of subtle terror, each with a unique twist. The stories unfold with a diverse cast of characters, all driven by a penchant for pushing boundaries. It's a tailor-made collection that is best enjoyed during the daylight hours!

The first story, '**Blackballed**,' introduces an arrogant pool player who meets his match in the form of two teenage girls on a mission to teach him a lesson on how to *really* play. From there, we delve into **'86,'** following the protagonist as she navigates the intriguing world of a Thai massage parlour with a unique menu featuring numbered massages. When she encounters the number 86, an unexpected twist unfolds. Next is the spooky tale '**Deja Brew**,' where a pensioner becomes convinced his wife is having an affair, unaware that her lover departed long ago. In '**Twisted**,' we peer through the eyes of a husband seeking to rekindle his youth when he encounters an old-school flame at a wedding. The collection concludes with **'La Oubliette Noir**,' tackling themes of revenge and justice as those who escape the law finally receive their just desserts.

Read the captivating first part of **'Blackballed'** and discover the chilling ending awaiting you in the rest of the collection.

Blackballed

Brad and Patsy argued all evening after he leered at Jan in her old-style waitress's uniform and fishnet stockings at the barbecue. Patsy even noticed him licking his lips and staring at her in the rear-view mirror. Brad thought she didn't know, that she couldn't tell. After they dropped Jan off at home, they had a confrontation in the street because he outright denied it. Sulking, he suggested they go home too, but she knew it would end badly. She looked at him with bloodshot eyes and told him she wanted to play pool, as she couldn't bear the thought of him harassing her for sex.

When they arrived at the pool hall, he parked outside. Upon entering, Brad scanned the room for the best table and paid. Stuffing a bulging wallet into his back pocket, he threw his keys at Patsy, and she placed them in her bag. With chalk and balls in one hand and drinks in the other, he spotted two girls a few tables away, one with a pony hawk and the other with a bob cut. He beamed from ear to ear. Brad loved an audience, especially young females. After chalking his cue and racking the balls, he theatrically rolled up the sleeves of an imaginary shirt.

An explosive crack sent the balls spinning all over the table. A coloured one slid into a side pocket. Brad bent to check before sinking another. Patsy scowled as he paced around the table, his spindly legs fuelled by enthusiasm. She visualised conking him on the forehead with the white ball to teach him a lesson.

Brad positioned himself with one foot on the floor and the other hanging off the table. Then he stepped back and frowned – using the cue to work out the angles, which Patsy found annoying. She knew he only did it for the sake of his prepubescent fans. Brad pulled the cue back but hesitated. Finally, he pulled back the cue again and struck the white ball, then potted his first, second, third, and fourth.

"Can you believe it?" he said, chalking the cue. Then, he missed the next shot. Patsy smirked, and her face turned a bit red. She started sweating and sat at the table, blotting with tissue. Then she took a swig of Southern Comfort and Red Bull, but it didn't seem to be working; it only enhanced the rage, causing her to miss the cue ball on her next shot. Brad stifled giggles, but when he missed his shot, she thanked God under her breath. When it was her turn, she stepped up to the table all business-like, trying to make up for lost ground. She potted one, then another. In the space of a few minutes, the tide turned, and she made a series of impressive fluky shots but acted as though they were intended. While she was on a roll, Brad looked red and mad as hell. From the corner of her eye, Patsy could see his brain working, figuring out a way to foil her. He started.

"What you wanna do after—"

"Stop trying to put me off!"

Then, it was all down to the black ball. Patsy walked around, trying to figure out the best angle. She positioned the cue on top of her shaky hand. At the same time, one of the other pool players responded to a goal on the widescreen television.

"One nil!"

Patsy jumped; her shot rebounded off the cushion and veered away from the pocket. Suddenly, Brad snatched his cue and chalked it, concentrating with his tongue sticking out to the side. After examining the tip, he positioned himself on the table, pulled back the cue, and sank the black ball.

Pony Hawk and Bob Cut cheered for him. Patsy cast a sharp glance their way and slammed her glass down on the table. Brad breezed around the pool table, glancing at the girls and flexing his biceps. When Pony Hawk winked at him, he met her gaze and reciprocated. At the same time, Bob Cut rolled her eyes towards the ceiling.

It was just after 9 pm when Patsy had had enough and wanted to go home. She could not deal with the flirting anymore. She told Brad she'd wait in the car for five minutes, and if he didn't come, he'd find her at home. It was either that or stay and serve him the cue in a very unnatural way and force a couple of stripes down his throat. Instead of going with her, he raised the stakes he would not be able to come back from. The girls watched intently, their smothered giggles drifting across the hall. As Patsy stormed out, Pony Hawk and Bob Cut eyed the door, checking to see if she'd really gone. After a while, they saw her speed off and moved in for the real game.

Brad took out a pound coin and rammed it into the slot. The balls clunked down into the mechanism under the table. Brad peered at Pony Hawk.

"Want Big Daddy to teach you some tricks, sexy?"

"I'm not very good," she smiled, glancing at Bob Cut, who rolled her eyes to the ceiling.

Brad licked his lips. "I'm sure I can teach you a thing or three."

Checking her out as she bent over the table, he moved in behind to guide her shot. She pressed backwards into him. Brad stood firm and didn't move. Minutes passed; he moved to the side, showing her how to make a bridge with her hand. After encouraging her to look down the cue as if holding a bow and arrow, she returned to her table and whispered something to Bob Cut. Again, Brad stared at Pony Hawk and winked. Then, after a slight pause, he reached beneath the table for the triangle. He racked up, placing stripes and spots correctly before positioning the black ball. He concentrated, tongue out to the side while he twisted the chalk on the end of his cue. Little did he know that it would be the last time he would twist anything, as an unexpected turn of events lurked just around the corner...

Other books by M. Henningham

This Deliciously Dark Short Story collection, featuring five tales of subtle terror, each with a unique and captivating twist. The stories unveil themselves with a diverse cast of characters, all propelled by a shared penchant for pushing boundaries. This tailor-made collection is best savored during the daylight hours!

The first story, "**Drunkface**," introduces us to a desperate youngster toying with the cord on a window blind. Delving deeper, we encounter the chilling narrative of "**Insane Reality**," where a pensioner's son loses his grip on sanity.
Moving forward, the spine-tingling tale "**Blood Moon**" unfolds, revealing a troubled mother crippled by internal conflict. In "**The Needling**," a wicked game of cat and mouse ensues, with needles as the weapons of choice. The collection concludes with "**The Great Rocco**," delving into themes of revenge and justice as a slick, Cockney gangster, who has eluded the law, finally faces magical karma and receives his just desserts."

DRUNKFACE

REVIEW:

COLDHEART – An image that stuck in my head long after I had finished reading.

'This book has five separate short stories, with varying themes and perspectives. I found that the first story was the most harrowing, and stuck with me throughout the book, although all are strong and unique. The "**Drunkface**" story was so well written though, I have not seen many short stories so quickly and fully immerse the reader, nor be as personal and hard hitting.
The author seamlessly transitions from first to third person perspectives, demonstrating great descriptive imagery from both styles of writing, making for a compelling collection of stories which have a genuine impact.'

Coming soon...

Honeydickers follows the daring exploits of three teenage grifters whose livelihood depends on the art of the steal. Their latest caper involves duping a detestable store owner in the depths of Hatton Garden, but little do they realize the gravity of their actions. News of their heist reaches the ears of a vengeful pursuer, propelling the trio to seek refuge in the sun-soaked escapism of Ibiza.

However, their quest for redemption turns sinister when they encounter a macabre, godlike figure lurking in the shadows. Undeterred by the supernatural aura surrounding this enigmatic being, the teens hatch a plan to rip him off, only to find themselves entangled in a web of divine wisdom.

As destinies collide and the thin line between justice, rebellion, and divine darkness blurs, chaos becomes the only constant. What unforeseen perils await these young grifters in this twisted dance of fate?

www.ingramcontent.com/pod-product-compliance
Lightning Source LLC
Chambersburg PA
CBHW040544170726
48295CB00012B/592